W9-AUE-965

WE GOT WORD THAT OUR FELLOW TEAMMATES WERE GETTING BUTCHERED A FEW MILES AWAY . . .

Eight PBRs pulled out loaded to the gunwales with killing power. I'll never forget the sight of Bernie holding his vintage .45 caliber grease gun, looking like he could chew raw meat. The rage etched in his camouflaged face epitomized the feeling of all of us. Ryan pulled out all the stops and raced out dual diesels at full RPM down the jungle-lined canal. We knew one of our boats was in the "Devil's Hole," but we didn't know if some of the crew members were still fighting for their lives . . .

I was in the forward .50 guntub when we screamed into the ambush site. Everyone onboard the PBRs was firing into the shoreline. Bullets cracked overhead like countless bullwhips. Stray rounds kicked up muddy geysers around our boats. The ominous *"sssssssss zzzzzzzzz whoooooo"* of an incoming RPG arced out of the jungle fringe, barely missing one of the boats. An enormous plume of water erupted, showering the PBR in sheets of river water. Inland, deadly blossoms of gray-black smoke burst through the sawgrass from the Navy Seawolf's rocket pods.

It was all over in minutes. Then all that was left was a deafening silence . . .

"No one can read *BEFORE THE DAWN* without seeing the true picture of the Vietnam War with all its battlefield horrors . . . The courage and sacrifices of American fighting men is reflected throughout . . . This book should be required reading for every American."
—Robinson Risner, Brigadier General, U.S.A.F., Retired, Former POW

Most Pocket Books are available at special quantity discounts for bulk purchases for sales promotions, premiums or fund raising. Special books or book excerpts can also be created to fit specific needs.

For details write the office of the Vice President of Special Markets, Pocket Books, 1230 Avenue of the Americas, New York, New York 10020.

BEFORE THE DAWN

Mickey Block
and
William Kimball

POCKET BOOKS

New York   London   Toronto   Sydney   Tokyo   Singapore

The accounts depicted in this book are factual and based on the true life experiences of Mickey Block. However, isolated details, locations, and names have been altered to protect the anonymity of the persons involved and safeguard the sensitive nature of certain incidents.

Mickey Block
U.S. Navy Petty Officer (Ret.)

POCKET BOOKS, a division of Simon & Schuster Inc.
1230 Avenue of the Americas, New York, NY 10020

Copyright © 1988 by Mickey Block
Cover art copyright © 1989 George Tsui

Published by arrangement with Daring Books

All rights reserved, including the right to reproduce
this book or portions thereof in any form whatsoever.
For information address Daring Books,
P. O. box 20-2050, Canton, OH 44701

ISBN: 0-671-72607-2

First Pocket Books printing June 1989

10 9 8 7 6 5 4 3 2

POCKET and colophon are registered trademarks of
Simon & Schuster Inc.

Printed in the U.S.A.

This book is dedicated to my deceased father,
a Forward Artillery Reconnaissance Officer,
1st Cavalry Division, New Guinea, 1943.
A man who longed to share so much
but had so little time. . . .

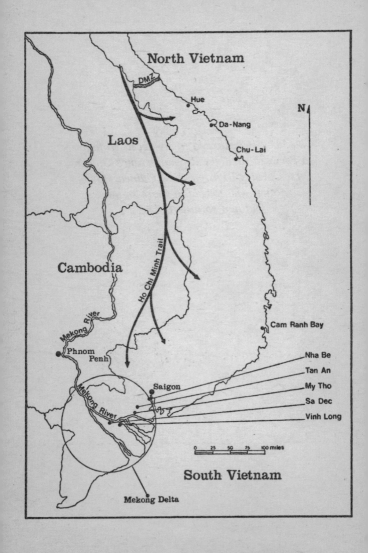

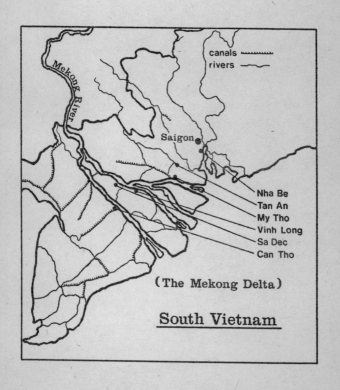

canals ·····················
rivers ——————

Mekong River

Saigon

Nha Be
Tan An
My Tho
Vinh Long
Sa Dec
Can Tho

(The Mekong Delta)

South Vietnam

Table of Contents

TABLE OF CONTENTS

Acknowledgments

I want to personally thank the young men who served in Vietnam as members of Special Boat Unit 524 and 573, SEAL Team One, and 5th Special Forces Group. Their commitment and sacrifices for freedom is unparalleled.

A note of sincere appreciation is due to Reverend Wayne and Kathy Benson and their ''special family'' of whom so many were used toward the healing of broken hearts and memories.

I also want to express my deepest indebtedness to Dave and Brenda Roever and the entire R.E.A. staff for their patience and commitment to our family and ministry.

And finally, I want to express my sincere love and gratitude to my wife Shirley and my children Jodi, Bryan, and Rocky for teaching me the true meaning of unconditional love.

Introduction

Scarlet tracers scratched fluorescent streaks through the blackness as soldiers fired blindly into the night. The confused cacophony of screaming men, machine guns and grenade concussions rent the pre-dawn darkness for a few deafening moments. Then it was over. An apprehensive silence followed, broken only by the mournful cries of wounded men.

In the distance I could hear the muffled whacking sound of an approaching chopper slapping through the moisture laden air. Someone had called in a dust-off. The resonant "dhup-dhup-dhup . . ." grew louder as the medevac neared. Against the acoustic backdrop of beating blades, the bulbous green hull angled in with its underbelly and tube skids flared as if she was breaking to stop.

I was hit bad and fighting for my life. I started to panic from a sudden feeling of suffocation. I couldn't breathe. My lungs were on fire and I was desperately gasping for air like a drowning man. I was in a dazed, trancelike stupor as I drifted close to shock. The pain was unbearable. My right leg was dangling in shreds from multiple bullet and shrapnel wounds. It felt like someone had hacked on it with an ax. I couldn't see what was happening as men carried me to the waiting chopper in a low crouch. Shrapnel from one of the explosions had peppered my face. I was bleeding profusely and the blood was draining into my eyes. I was terrified that I was blinded.

Under the relentless beating of the rotors, and the yells of the crew chief and corpsmen, I was heaved into the chopper bay next to Kenny. My body felt like liquid jelly as I floated in a warm pool of my own blood. I was dying, but I fought back the blackness that was closing in around me.

Everything was a confused collage of impressions: the slippery sensation of the blood smeared liner; the damp sticky feeling of bloody fatigues clinging to my body; the agile, probing hands of the medic; the tight, tearing feeling of a tourniquet; the vibration of the chopper as the pilot throttled down; the sickening sweet metallic taste of human blood.

The crew chief shouted something to the pilot. The doorgunner looked down with a stone cold expression on his face, then released the safety on his M-60. The blades screwed faster and faster as the engine torque mounted, whipping the scrub brush back and forth in the down draft. The Huey shifted nervously on its skids, tilted forward then climbed into the Vietnamese night.

I remember feeling the shudder of incoming rounds puncturing the thin skinned hull of the Huey as we banked over a treeline and the hellish sigh of glowing green fireballs floating up from the jungle in slow motion. The doorgunner was stuttering away as a brassy stream of spent casings piled up in disarray on the fluted floor of the chopper or tumbled into the night.

Under the din of the rotor blades, the buffeting night wind gusting through the open bay, and the frantic curses of the pilot, I could barely hear the wheezing, gurgling sound of Kenny lying next to me. I canted my head sideways and saw the reflection of his blood soaked chest in the dim cabin light, frothing with tiny pink bubbles from a sucking chest wound. He was groaning and writhing on the floor as the medic fought to stabilize both of us. As we floated above the deceptive tranquillity of mosaic paddy lands and jade colored jungle en route to the 3rd Field Hospital, I didn't know if either of us would make it. With my medical training, I knew we had a pretty good chance of survival if we could reach a skilled surgical team in time.

An eternity seemed to pass before the chopper banked into a graceful spiraling descent into Tan Son Nhut Airbase. I could just make out the shadows of Saigon and the sparkling lights of the city against the velvet blackness. The chopper glided toward the landing pad in a steep, fast descent before hitting with a rough jar that sent sharp pains stabbing through my body like hot pokers.

The blades tapered off to a slow whacking spin as the gunner let the barrel of the 60 droop toward the ground, and the medic maneuvered around the blood splattered bay in preparation to unload. I could hear the whine of jeep transmissions as they downshifted to a stop. Several medics grabbed me and lifted me onto a stretcher mounted on the tailend of the jeep. My whole body was screaming in pain as they secured me then sped across the tarmac.

I was half lucid, half incoherent as a barrage of confused images raced by in a blur: the warm propblast of the Huey, the hollow slapping sound of the slow spinning blades, the sweet smell of kerosene from the engine exhaust, the bark of orders, the twinkling yellow lights in the distance, the grinding of gears, and the freezing cold sensation of wet fatigues as we raced across the runway.

The jeep screeched to a stop in front of an anxious covey of medical personnel who lifted me onto a gurney and wheeled me into the hospital. I remember doctors and nurses silhouetted against the bright corridor lights frantically shouting medical instructions as we burst through the double doors into the emergency room.

The pain was excruciating. The chopper medic had tied off the arterial bleeding on my right leg, but I had lost a tremendous amount of blood. My blood pressure had fallen dangerously low and most of my veins had collapsed. They were struggling to insert an I.V. of life saving blood in time.

My camouflaged fatigues were drenched in sweat and red-black blood which had already begun to coagulate in places, but blood was still seeping from multiple punctures and what was left of my legs.

The doctors were frantically cutting away my sticky fatigues and mud-caked jungle boots with surgical scissors. Time was running out. They knew that they were going to lose this young commando if they didn't hurry. Precious seconds lay between me and eternity.

A nurse was wiping blood from my eyes when I noticed a Catholic Chaplain hovering over me like the Grim Reaper. He had a satin colored sash draped around his neck and was anointing my forehead with oil. He was solemnly administering Last Rites: "May the Lord forgive you my son by this Holy anointing whatever sins you have committed . . ." with an open palm, he made the sign of the cross, then backed away. His presence could only mean that I was dying . . .

1

The Sins of The Fathers

Those who passed through the long night of 'Nam and still linger in its shadows know above all how painful the ordeal; how deep the wound. In war, some men receive flesh wounds while others are afflicted with more subtle scars. Some came home from Vietnam in flag-draped coffins, some disfigured without arms or legs or eyes, while untold thousands returned psychologically shattered—whole in body but broken in spirit, a quiet company of men and women wounded within.

The visible injuries are much easier to perceive, but the hidden wounds of the heart and soul are often more difficult to diagnose and harder to heal. During the Vietnam Conflict, a steady stream of unseen casualties trickled home as anonymous servicemen in transit, lugging the residual baggage of war. At a casual glance, they appeared no different than the ever present ebb tide of men in uniform who seem so natural a part of airport lobbies or bus terminals. But to the discerning observer, there was something different about their eyes.

Outwardly, they may not have manifested the 1,000 yard

stare of shell-shocked soldiers straggling back to the rear after grim months of combat, but still, their haggard eyes revealed something deeper, something haunting. They were often darker and older and pained. They were windows to the troubled soul of a wounded generation of adolescent men. They were eyes which betrayed a loss of innocence and a look of knowing beyond their years.

I was one of those who returned both crippled in body and soul. But for me, the physical and emotional wounds cut deeper than the steaming jungles and paddy lands of 'Nam. They reached back to the earliest memories of my childhood.

Beyond the fact that I was born in Marion, Indiana on August 2, 1947 as Michael Yankovich and have a brother and four sisters whom I have never met, I remember little of my first two years.

But, I do bear the marbled scars on my back from the glowing heads of cigarettes crushed into my tender flesh and the traumatic memories of a monstrous face with a bulging eye which reoccurred in terrifying nightmares until I left for Vietnam. I later learned from a psychiatrist that it stemmed from the fragile impressions of a tiny baby as my biological parents leaned over the crib, grabbed me and screamed in my face.

As a result of the early child abuse, I was taken into the custody of the Child Protection Agency. I was placed in an orphanage at the age of two, where I spent six months before being adopted.

I still retain misty memories of my mother's arrival at the orphanage to receive me, and the comforting sight of her warm smile and outstretched arms.

After she drove me home, she gave me a bath, dressed me in a pair of new pajamas, and told me to go say goodnight to my adoptive father. My first impressions of the man were laced with terror. Lying on the living room sofa was a stern looking hulk of a man. His clumsy attempts to pet me on the head triggered all the pent-up fears of a

18

brutalized boy. I instinctively covered my face and screamed. The sight of his enormous hands reaching toward me was a signal of impending pain. It was the fearful reaction of a toddler who had been conditioned by alcoholic parents who thought nothing of slamming my body against a wall, pushing me down a flight of stairs, or blistering my baby flesh with burning cigarettes.

My adopted parents sought to comfort me with assurances that those experiences were now in the past. Still, in spite of their sincerity, I never really felt like I belonged. In their misguided ignorance, they unintentionally made me feel inferior. Years later, when they bore their own children, I was always introduced to friends and acquaintances as their "adopted" son, while my stepbrothers were introduced as their "natural" children. I know they meant it innocently, but I grew up feeling like a second class son who was not quite as good as their real sons. It seemed as though I never quite attained the status of a full-fledged member of the family.

From my earliest years, an enormous burden was unconsciously placed upon my shoulders by parents who meant well but tragically failed to perceive the oppressive weight of their expectations. They felt that I was destined, or bound, to achieve great things because I had been so fortunate to have been plucked out of such a dead end situation.

I grew up with their reminders that out of a cast of thousands, they had selected me, and I should be eternally indebted to have been chosen out of all the masses of forsaken kids. Whether they meant to or not, I was led to feel that I owed them; that I should somehow repay their supreme act of benevolence; that the sum total of my life was bound to measure up to their great expectations.

Even so, my mother endeavored to reassure me that I was no different. For her, I was loved on an equal footing with her real children. My mother was a wonderful woman. At a petite 5'1", she was dwarfed in my father's presence. She was a product of her times, nurtured by sacrifice, fear and duty. My adoptive parents were from the Class of '40. They had weathered the firestorm of Hitler's Reich and the Rising Sun. They had emerged from the global bloodbath to pick up the pieces of their lives and resume the quest for the American dream.

In the black and white commercials of the late forties, my mom was the dutiful Donna Reed wife wearing a spotless sundress, standing by the white picket fence waiting for her husband to come home from work with his lunch pail. She was the submissive wife with a heart of gold who had sacrificed on the home front while her man slugged it out in the South Pacific. She was a fiercely loyal woman who sought only to reward her mate with undying love for his service overseas. She asked little in return. Her single-minded purpose was to serve my father while he ruled the house with a fist of iron. Whatever he did, right or wrong, she was duty bound to stand by his side.

Even when my stepfather would lash out at me in sudden outbursts of anger, she held her peace. I knew that it tore her up emotionally, but she was too afraid or just too loyal to oppose him. Even to this day, she has so repressed the memories that she cannot bring herself to admit they ever happened.

Our relationship had been very close. Maybe I was drawn to her warmth to compensate for the lack of affection I received from my father, or maybe she was unconsciously compensating for his inability to express love. At times, she seemed to go out of her way to spoil me by buying me little things. When I was a toddler, she would change me three times a day and sewed little suits to dress me up. My dad would mildly reprimand her because he felt she was spoiling me so much that one day I would be unable to cope with the inevitable.

When my body was butchered in 'Nam, it devastated my mother. She didn't know how to handle it. While my father's response was a predictable, "Well, if we feel sorry for him, he'll wallow in self-pity for the rest of his life and never amount to anything, so we're going to act like it was no big deal that he lost a leg and a hand." The "bite the bullet" philosophy which typified my father's attitude was, "Be tough, take the pain, and suffer like a man." As far as he was concerned, men didn't shed tears unless they were sissies.

My father was the sort of man who commanded respect. When he entered a room of people the unspoken response was, "Who is that guy?" At an imposing 6'2" and weighing 275 pounds plus, he exuded an aura of uncontested strength. He was one of those men who intimidated people without trying. He too was a product of his times. The deprivations of the Great Depression and the anxious uncertainties of World War II left an indelible stamp upon my father which he shouldered until his grave.

He was of proud Hollander stock, raised in a religious family, in a staunch brand of Calvinism. His heritage was deeply ingrained with the Protestant work ethic whose virtues were reinforced through the dark years of the depression. He was a child of the "hungry thirties." By the age of ten he was hustling the streets and markets of old Grand Rapids selling papers and doing odd jobs to scrape by. But such was his drive and determination that he became a successful salesman during the lean, postwar years and eventually, president of his own company.

But much of my father's temperament was conditioned by his combat experiences as a young soldier in the South Pacific.

He received his draft notice shortly after the Japanese attack on Pearl Harbor. He was barely twenty. He went in the army as a private, but because of his leadership abilities, he was put through O.C.S. and commissioned a brown bar lieutenant. He was an artillery officer who fought with the 1st Cavalry Division in the jungles of New Guinea and the island hopping campaigns of MacArthur. He even volunteered for a torturous stint with the famed

Merril's Marauders in Burma. When his company commander and the executive officer were killed he ended up assuming the command of nearly 200 men at the ripe old age of twenty-two. Except for a handful who walked out, most of his men were killed in the South Pacific.

I seldom saw my father drink. It wasn't that he hated the taste of alcohol, he simply feared the rage which he kept bottled up inside. He was more afraid of what he was capable of if he lost control. Looking back, I can see that he brought part of the war back with him. There may not have been any naked symptoms, but those of us who have journeyed to hell and back know the private pathos that can be carried home.

It wasn't just his temperament that caused my father to develop ulcers. Countless forays into Japanese garbage dumps at night to steal tainted scraps of food which rotted out his stomach, acidic nerve-wracking years of suspense, and the ever present fear of death exerted tremendous pressures upon men's minds and nerves.

In the crucible of fire and fear and blood, men can be tempered and hardened and sometimes marred. My father was a different man when he returned. Four gut-wrenching years of purgatory had blunted the senses and left their brutal imprint upon his spirit.

I remember the halting cadence in his voice as he told a telling story of one sweaty night in the jungle. It was one of those hot and sticky nights when fatigues were soaked with nervous sweat; when night blackness played tricks with men's eyes; when specters of fear toyed with fertile imaginations. It was one of those sweltering jungle nights when the stagnant smells of sour sweat, damp earth, and rotting vegetation hung heavy in the humid air. The tension was palpable as anxious men huddled in sodden foxholes waiting out another worried night. Ears pricked at every sound, straining for subtle disturbances in the jungle's ambience. But nothing moved. A dark sense of foreboding hung over the jungle like an ominous refrain.

Except for the labored breathing of tense soldiers, the jungle was still. Then from somewhere in the clotted tangle of snarled vines and lush foliage came the bloodcurdling screams of a captured G.I. Jolts of adrenaline stabbed through men dug in along the line. To the man, they shared the same unspoken nightmare being played out by a captured comrade. The Japs had staked him out a couple hundred yards up the ridge and were methodically torturing him. His agonizing cries for help only heightened that cold, blind, anonymous sense of fear which stalked the lines at night.

The company had been whittled down dangerously low, making a rescue attempt sheer suicide. Besides, the Japs were night wise, dug in with machine guns waiting to cut down any Americans who were foolhardy enough to come thrashing through the thick jungle in the inky blackness. But he just kept screaming and begging, "Please God, please. Kill me . . . somebody shoot me for God's sake!"

So my father called in an artillery salvo to silence the torment. In moments, the guttural sound of freight-training shells rushed overhead before ripping the jungle with violent seizures of fire and steel. Blizzards of red-hot shrapnel sliced through vines and broad leaves and flesh. When the resonant concussions died out, my father was left with a leaden silence which weighed heavy upon his conscience for the rest of his life.

It wasn't long afterward that he learned that his best friend had been tortured to death in a similar fashion. That's when something snapped inside. Maybe it was the agonizing depth of frustration and helplessness. Or maybe it was the oppressive guilt of knowing he made it back when so many others had not.

He was twenty-two pushing fifty in his mind. He finally picked up a severe strain of malaria which lashed his body with feverish, cramping bouts that threatened to kill him. For over a year, he fought a desperate battle to survive in the Fort Custer Hospital in Battle Creek, Michigan. It was his gutsy will to survive that seemed to pull him through. It was that tenacious determination that governed the course of his life. He was a self-made man whose philosophy was, "You are what you have, and what you have is what you get. You show me a good loser, and I will show you a loser!"

My father had hoped to make the military a career, but his ambitious quest to be a general by his forties was cut short by the recurring bouts of malaria. After his discharge, he returned to Grand Rapids to start over with my mom. However, their plans to build a family were soon frustrated by their inability to conceive children. Chris and Terry were natural sons who came as surprises a decade later, but after the first fruitless years of trying, they settled for second best. I was adopted in 1950 and my younger brother Mark was adopted a couple years later.

What was particularly galling was the fact that my father's brother and sister were having kids like they were coming off of an assembly line. When viewed against my father's view of masculinity, you weren't a man unless you sired four or five kids. This was a tragic ingredient that played into the feelings of inferiority fostered by my father; after all, I wasn't flesh of his flesh or the proof of his manhood. To compensate for this perceived inadequacy, he strove to make me into the image he desired me to be. I was the raw material from which he purposed to fashion the baseball pro, the college grad that he could never be. Not that he was stupid, he just never had the opportunities to cultivate his brilliant mind.

But I found his demands an oppressive burden to bear. I tried so hard to measure up, but the task was impossible—like trying to drive back the ocean with a push broom. Every time I failed, I was made to feel how much I had let him down, especially in light of all he had done to deliver me from the orphanage and take me in.

Until I went to 'Nam, I strove to prove myself, strove to win his approval, strained to please him. People would comment, "Oh, so you're the son your father's always talking about," as if to acknowledge some special breeding. Dad would brag to others about me and tell them how proud he was and how much he loved me, but he never told me. I cannot remember ever hearing my father say, "I love you." Maybe it was because he didn't know how to love. Maybe he had never loved himself. Maybe he had never learned from his father before him.

He expressed his love by providing financial security or buying you something. But I didn't want things. I didn't yearn for material tokens of his affection. I simply wanted his affection. So I grew up endeavoring to earn his love. I respected his strength and esteemed his abilities, but what I longed for was his acceptance, his support, and most of all his love.

It was in this confused tapestry of human shortcomings and silent tension that the frayed fabric of my life was interwoven.

After the war, my father built a small house on a few acres out in the country which his grandfather had sold him. I think his grandfather felt the pastoral setting would help soothe the wounds. Until we moved to Grand Rapids when I was eight, my bouts with child abuse were a sporadic, hit or miss affair. But after moving into the city, the incidents grew more severe.

The subsurface stress which had been boiling inside for years finally began to surface in unpredictable flashes of anger. It was the same strain of delayed stress which I, myself, was destined to carry home from 'Nam. It was a festering abscess of guilt and rage which can poison the mind and slowly kills unless it is lanced and drained.

His outbursts of anger were rooted in a repressed past— a past that had been gaining on him for years. Looking back, it seemed that he had quietly struggled to stay one step ahead of it, but he had fought too long and was just too wearied to shake those haunting phantoms of the soul.

So I became the occasional whipping boy who bore the

brunt of his frustration. It was a frustration directed as much at himself as it was to me. Maybe it was because we were not so very different after all. I was the mirror who reflected all the disappointment he had come to despise in himself.

With the passing of time wounds are healed and bitter memories mellowed. He rarely apologized for the pain he inflicted, but in the clarity of hindsight, I think he agonized, even grieved in the privacy of his heart for something he desperately wanted to master but instead mastered him. I know this now, but at the time I was a child who lived with a siege mentality, half-cowering under the specter of fear and reprisal.

By the time I entered the 5th grade, I started discharging blood from my rectum. The doctor diagnosed me as having an ulcer. Medication was prescribed to calm my nerves, but it did little to relieve the relentless pressure to succeed.

Ironically, that very pressure accomplished just the opposite in me. Few can flourish in an atmosphere of fear and criticism, so I became a mediocre student. Not only did I feel like an idiot, but the caustic reminders of my stupidity only deepened my sense of inferiority.

The only thing I halfway excelled at was sports. But even there, my good was never quite good enough. My ineptitude finally triggered the pent-up frustration of my father in one violent outburst of rage. I was twelve when it happened. Our little league team was 17-1 that season with me as the star pitcher. My father had told me to come right home after the game to babysit my younger brothers so my mother and he could attend an office picnic out at Lake Michigan.

The ball park was quite a ways from home so I caught a ride with one of my buddies and his parents. It was their custom to stop off at an ice cream parlor on the way back to celebrate our winning streak. I knew that my dad wanted me home, but I figured a few minutes savoring the spoils of our victory wouldn't matter. Well, I figured wrong.

When I walked through the front door, all was quiet. But, I couldn't miss the loaded picnic basket lying ominously in the hallway. The next few moments are frozen in my mind. They are as clear to me today as if they happened only yesterday. My father strode into the living room and demanded to know where I had been. I remember the surge of adrenaline and the pounding pulsebeat of my chest, when I sarcastically tried to explain that Bucky Sanders' folks had stopped off at the ice cream parlor on the way back, and we had come home as soon as they were done.

All I remember was the blurred sight of his huge right hand, a sharp pain in my nose, then everything went black. The next thing I realized was my back arched over the kitchen sink with the faucet splashing cold water into my upturned face. I remember gagging and spitting up blood and saliva, and the drowning sensation as water poured into my nose. My mother was yelling at my father because blood had been splattered all over her new living room carpet.

They finished washing my face and handed me a wet towel to hold over my nose. They told me to watch my baby brother, then they left for the picnic.

My head was throbbing from the excruciating pain. I must have been bordering on shock because all I wanted to do was close my eyes and sleep. But I didn't dare sleep. I was terrified what my father would do if he came home and found me asleep. I feared he would kill me.

I patted my face and could tell it was puffy. My skin felt like a water balloon. I went into a small bathroom off the kitchen to see how bad I looked. When I flicked on the light, I could barely see. The bridge of my nose and eye sockets were engorged with blood. They had turned a purplish blue and were nearly swollen shut. I looked like Rocky Balboa at the start of the fifteenth round.

After hours of anxious foreboding, the flash of head-lights and the sounds of a car pulling into the driveway announced my parents' return. When they walked into the living room, the sight of my face stopped them in their tracks. Even my father was stunned. My mother grimaced, put her hand to her mouth, and abruptly left the room. She couldn't handle it. Maybe she was afraid she would say something to my father.

I was lying on the davenport with my face a grotesque caricature of my former self. My father slumped into his big chair with an exhausted sigh. He sheepishly said, "Come here and sit on my lap." There was sorrow and defeat in his voice, but I didn't flinch. I didn't know whether to trust him. I could sense that he was choking up. There were no tears, even though all the tears of a lifetime wanted to spill out. "Please, come and sit on my lap." The tone in his voice was no longer authoritative or demanding. It was almost pleading, as if in some tragic way we each sensed that something had died between us.

He came over and cradled me in his arms and propped me on his lap. Almost inaudibly, I heard him swallow and choke back the tremor of emotion. "You know, son, sometimes your dad has a bad temper. It doesn't happen all the time, but sometimes things happen that make me lose my temper." He was struggling to cope with his emotions and find words to express himself. "I never meant to hit you as hard as I did. I swear that I will never hit you again."

But I was much too numb and too bitter to believe him now. He desperately wanted me to hug him, but I couldn't bring myself to do it. The hurt was just too deep. He kept repeating that he would never strike me again. But I knew that things wouldn't change, and they didn't. The physical abuse finally tapered off when I entered high school. By then he was fought out. He had resigned himself to the fact I was a lost cause. So he just gave up trying. Besides, he now had other boys to raise.

2

Come On All Of You Big Strong Men

If there was ever a celluloid version of my father he was aptly characterized in the film, "The Great Santini." He too was a regimented, hard-driving, perfection ist who couldn't tolerate weakness in others—especially his eldest son. I either excelled under his roof or I got out.

I was such a dismal scholastic failure by my senior year that my chances of making it academically carried about as much hope of success as nailing jelly to the wall. As far as my father was concerned, it didn't take a lot of discernment to see that I wasn't Harvard material. I was never going to be a brain surgeon or corporate lawyer or baseball pro for that matter. I was Mickey Block, high school flunky and adolescent screw up.

Outside of skipping classes and hanging out at the beach, I had no motivation my senior year. I was grounded most of the time because my grades were so pathetic. Teenagers are reminded that their senior year is supposed to be the best time of their life, but it was more like a prison lockdown to me. I figured that if I was going to be grounded from going out at night, why waste my days studying. I was just biding my time until I escaped.

As graduation day approached, I was confronted with the sobering possibility that I wouldn't graduate. I got caught blowing off locker doors with M-80's at the high school. They didn't want to carry me for another year any more than my father did, so they made me do penance by cleaning wads of chewing gum off of all the empty seats in the school. I spent ten days in June earning my final right of passage from the Class of '66.

My father was half relieved, half elated that I had gotten my diploma. He could see the light at the end of the tunnel. In a few months, I would be out of the house and no longer an embarrassing albatross around his neck. That's why he encouraged me to join up, but maybe deep down inside he entertained one last fleeting ray of hope that the military would make a man out of me yet. If I could amount to something, anything in the service, at least he could say I was in the military learning a trade, doing something patriotic for my country. Besides, he would have completely disowned me if I had graduated from high school, let my hair grow, stuck a flower in my ear and hitchhiked to San Francisco.

My cousin Roger was drafted into the army and shipped to Vietnam while I was finishing my senior year. My father was proud of him because he went out of a sense of duty and honor. Even though there had been a healthy competitiveness between us growing up, which was encouraged by my father and his brother, my cousin and I were close friends. I remember sitting at the kitchen table one morning after Roger had left for Vietnam. I was very much aware of Vietnam. It seemed to take on an almost ominous quality during our senior year. Besides, you couldn't pick up the paper or watch Walter Cronkite without seeing jungle boots protruding from poncho liners, dust-offs, and weekly body counts. I knew teenage soldiers were getting wasted half a world away, but I was still too far removed from the death and dying to comprehend the lethal impact of it all.

When I made some off-handed crack that I didn't think it took a lot of brains to go somewhere where you were going to get shot up, my father came unglued. He grabbed me from across the table and screamed in my face, ''Don't you ever say anything rotten about guys going into the service, or serving their country, no matter what happens to them . . . besides you'll never measure up to what Roger is doing for his country!''

Maybe in some warped way my father's outburst helped provoke me into enlisting. Deep down inside I still wanted to prove myself. I still entertained a measure of hope that I could make my father proud of me. The service seemed like the answer. Besides, I relished the idea of joining up. I too was steeped in the same wave-the-flag, apple pie, motherhood, ''guns, guts and glory'' patriotism that my father so fondly cherished.

During the last semester of my senior year Rod Walker, one of my close buddies who was sort of a ''Fonzarelli'' type, talked me into joining the Navy with an impressive argument that they had better looking uniforms. In a mock show of bravado I mouthed off that I wanted to go Airborne and join the Green Berets, without having the slightest idea of what it would involve. But after talking to Rod, romantic visions of sea duty won me over. It was ''Go Navy and see the World!'' We decided to join up on the ''buddy system'' which guaranteed that we would go through basic training together.

Neither of us told our parents that we had gone to the recruiter. It wasn't that I was sneaking around behind their backs in defiance . . . I just assumed they would be so excited when I broke the news. I remember coming home with a gloating look of self-satisfaction, like the cat that swallowed the canary. I had finally done something right.

I found my dad sitting at the kitchen table. ''Dad, I got something to tell you. I just went down to the recruiter's office and signed up for the Navy.'' I didn't expect him to respond the way he did. Without warning, he lunged out of his chair, grabbed me by the shoulders, and shoved me against the wall. He released his grip. ''You'll never make it in the service, you can't even stand at attention. You aren't tough enough.'' Half turning, he swiped my midsection with his forehand and added, ''You can't even hold your stomach in.'' I remember my mom's protest, maybe because they were so rare; ''Oh Honey, knock it off, he's only a kid.'' With just a hiss of disgust in his voice, he responded, ''He thinks he's so tough because he's going in the Navy. If he ever gets sent to someplace like Vietnam he won't cut it.''

The wind was completely taken out of my sails. I had been so convinced that he would be pleased. It just drove the wedge deeper between us.

Looking back, I now know that he did not intend to come off the way he did. It was his clumsy way of preparing me. After all, I wasn't joining the Boy Scouts. He had lost his youth overseas and that near mythical illusion of immortality so coveted by youthful men. He knew how the delicate idealism of youth could be shattered, the conscience raped, and the nobility of man twisted and tried by war.

In his own crude way, my father was mimicking the demanding, never satisfied drill sergeant who barked and criticized and threatened. It was not out of some perverted display of power, but because he knew how the flower of youth could be crushed before its time and sought to prepare me for what was to come.

He knew I was about to embark upon that pilgrimage from which there is often no return. He had taken that pilgrimage in his youth and had come back, but he knew the savagery of combat, the naked perversity of war, and the unbearable sacrifices it can impose. In his own awkward way he was trying to say, ''It will take everything you have and then some.''

But, at the time, I didn't discern any empathy between a father and a son. I only saw more rejection. It simply reinforced my determination to get out.

A few days later, Rod and I were given food vouchers by the recruiters and herded onto a chartered bus for our induction physicals in Detroit. We shared the ride with a busload of teenagers—some with blank vacant looks, others with nervous grins whose sole combat experiences consisted of nothing more than fighting zits, their girl-friends, or high school finals. Beyond the athletic clash of a scrimmage line, the gamey maneuvers of dating, or the stoplight duels of '57 Chevys on Friday night, we were novices at playing war. Our notions of war had been crafted by John Wayne and "Back to Bataan," plastic soldiers, Mattel rifles, and Vic Morrow every Tuesday night at 7:30, fighting his way across France in "Combat."

We had no idea what lay on the horizon. Some showed no discernible apprehension, while others manifested the telltale faces of grim resignation. Some were enjoying their first tenative steps to independence. To them, it was the beginning of a great adventure.

But for most, the Selective Service had interrupted their teenage rhythms. They were sentenced to a two-year stretch in the Green Machine with the prospects of death or maiming a distinct possibility. Less than half of us were red, white and blue patriots who wanted to serve our country. The majority were reluctant conscripts who had lost deferments and were drafted because their freedom had run out. Some had waited fatalistically for the inevitable notice to arrive from their local draft board. They didn't have the money or the grades for college, or the clout to manipulate a deferment. Others had tried everything under the sun to avoid the draft but failed. They were just too cowardly or conscientious to cross the border. Others prayed for a miraculous, eleventh hour reprieve in the form of a 4F classification. And finally, the realists among us simply hoped that when all was said and done, they would not end up a grunt.

My greatest fear was that I would be found ineligible and medically unfit. I don't think I could have taken the humiliation. It would have been the ultimate disgrace in my father's eyes. Besides, I desperately wanted to qualify. I had to get out. I wanted to do something with my life. I didn't want to slowly wither and waste away in some dead end job in Grand Rapids. It seemed that history was passing me by and I longed to be a part of it. I fantasized about telling my friends someday that I was where the action had been.

At the induction center in Detroit, we were ordered to undress and were issued hospital gowns and paper slippers to begin our day long battery of physical and psychiatric exams. We shuffled like mindless automatons down endless corridors following a labyrinth of pastel paths painted on linoleum floors. They led us through a humiliating litany of bending, coughing, spreading, poking and urinating. There was something dehumanizing about the whole experience. We weren't men with names and emotions and fears, but cattle in the chute. We were numbers, entries on a clipboard, test scores, medical profiles, cannon fodder. The bedside manner of the examining physicians didn't help. Their matter-of-fact indifference was that of stockmen segregating sheep for the packing house. Along the line some fell out, diagnosed with flat feet, perforated ear drums, color blindness, high blood pressure, asthma, poor hearing, bad eyes, bad blood and bad urine. Some took it hard, others received the news as if they had won the lottery. But most of us qualified whether we wanted to or not. I just kept progressing down the little painted trails from one station to the next until I completed them all. I had passed with a 1A classification.

At the end, they lined us up in a row and an officer arbitrarily selected us like umsympathetic SS officers at Dachau; segregating unsuspecting Jews from the cattle cars for the showers or the work camps. "You, you and you are in the Marines, the rest go to the Army." I was overjoyed that I had already signed up for the Navy. I took the bus home to graduate and party out the summer until I shipped off to boot camp in August.

My final months as a civilian were not fraught with anxieties. I wasn't going to fight the Cong, I was going in the Navy. The closest I'd ever get to Vietnam was several safe miles offshore, floating on the sparkling blue-greens of the South China Sea. I was going on a ship to exotic ports of call, to Japan, Hong Kong, Rome, Buenos Aires, the Golden Gate. It was going to be a cruise—one long party. I was finally going to see the world. It was going to be nothing but "booze and tattoos" for this kid.

The pressure was lifted that summer as my buddies and I played out our version of "Happy Days." Even my father didn't hassle me to get a job. He just let me kick back and savor the last days of my youth.

We spent the summer knocking around high school haunts and drinking beers on the sand dunes at Lake Michigan; soaking up the sun and summer breezes. It was a frivolous time of cruising around in an open convertible, smoking cigarettes and acting like carefree fools.

We were poised at the crossroads of adolescence and manhood. It was "American Graffiti"—the sentimental end of an era. It was a time of rending; when we would be torn in different directions. We wanted to go and yet linger at the same time, like the first hesitant steps of an infant who's not quite confident enough to let go of his mother's hand.

Growing up was pulling us apart. Wayne was going to work in a large supermarket when he received his draft notice. Rick was so freaked that he was going to get drafted that he enlisted in the Naval Reserves. Jimmy was packing for Purdue in the fall. Our boyhood camaraderie was unraveling. The bond was being broken. We swore nothing would change, as if we were blood brothers taking a sacred vow of allegiance, but we all knew in our hearts that it was coming to a close. Fate was sending us on our separate ways.

There was a lot of nostalgic small talk the summer of '66. We all swore to write and tell each other what it was like, but we didn't know what we were talking about. We magnified our sexual prowess and bragged about going to Hong Kong and seeing the babes, but there was always a faint trace of timidity in our boasts. We were still innocent, wet behind the ears, and virgins. We knew little of forbidden pleasures or the ways of the world. We had never smoked a joint. A doper to us was some faggot in New York. We knew we weren't kids anymore, and we tried to act grown-up, but an unspoken nervousness and trepidation permeated our conversations.

Guys would boast of kicking rear and killing "gooks," but we knew nothing of what it would be like to lie face down in the fermenting muck of a rice paddy with your own hot blood draining from an open stomach or to realize you were dying under the blistering brilliance of a Vietnamese sun 12,000 miles from your home and friends, who had sat with you on top of the dunes listening to "Surfer Girl" and "Yesterday." It was a time of calm before the storm.

As my summer escapism was drawing to a close, our church bulletin had an announcement that they were accepting membership into the church on a profession of faith. Each year they held a candlelight procession for seniors who were willing to enter the rolls of the church. It was a liturgical coming of age, a religious circumcision, a Presbyterian equivalent to bar mitzvah.

I'd followed my parents to church all my life, attended a parochial high school and endured catechism classes on Wednesday night with the scrupulousness of a pharisee, but I had been more involved with the social trappings of church life than committed with any depth of devotion. I thought you could join the church like joining the YMCA or 4H. I had been thoroughly indocrinated in the tenets of Christianity, but in my ignorance I had concluded that "joining the church" unconditionally reserved for me a one-way ticket to heaven when I died.

My parents weren't dumping any condemnation on me to accept my passage into eternal security, but the peer pressure was enormous. All my friends were doing it. If you didn't do it, it was like not going to your prom, or even worse, you ran the risk of being marked as an atheist or unpatriotic pagan. I told my mom that I wasn't sure about making "the profession" for church membership, but in the end the social pressure won out. Besides, I was going in the service and a little edge wouldn't hurt. I had just enough fear of God to see the prudence in taking out a religious life insurance policy just in case providence sent me to 'Nam.

But there was more to my reticence than the question of practicality. There was just enough superstition in me to justify the need for religious symbols and lucky talismans like crucifixes, St. Christopher medals, and phylacteries; but I knew deep down inside that true religion required the heart and not merely lip service, and my heart wasn't in it. I didn't see enough redeeming value in being "churched" to say, "This is what I want for my life." There was a lot of religious window dressing and piousity in the church, but it was often a religious veneer which camouflaged a lot of hypocrisy.

I would go along with the formality of it all if it would please Mom and Dad, placate my friends, and confer some mystical mantel of divine favor. But, beyond that, I had little interest in religion. I remember being brought before the governing body of the church consisting of twelve men and the Pastor. He was an absurd cross between a Sears and Roebuck hippy and clerical nerd. He had long hair, smoked a pipe, and advocated the gospel of "If it feels good, do it!"

I remember telling the inquisition in all honesty, "I

37

don't know if this is the right church for me, there are a lot of things I don't understand." They solemnly inquired if I believed in God and I said "yes." "Do you believe in Jesus?" "Yes." "Do you believe that he died for your sins?" "Yes." I felt like I was being given an oral exam for my driver's license. "Well, then the rest will come in time." That was that. I was given an honorary Bible and a round of handshakes as if I had been initiated into the local Moose Lodge or the Kiwanis. There weren't any hot flashes or tingling sensations or rapturous visions of the heavens rolling back with myriads of angels singing the "Hallelujah Chorus." But as far as the board was concerned, my name had been inscribed on the golden roll up yonder with indelible ink.

Now that God was in my hip pocket, my eternal destiny sealed, and God on my side, I would put it all behind me and live the rest of my life as I saw fit.

Good-byes are more melancholy in times of war than similar farewells in times of peace. They are different than good-byes when you leave for college or take a vacation or even wave to neighborhood friends when you move away. They become more than civil courtesies or parting formalities between acquaintances who know they will meet again. They assume a more somber and searching quality than would be necessary during more passive seasons of life. It stems from the unspoken understanding that farewells in time of war may be forever.

My first farewells were said in silence to the mementos of my youth, to the sanctuary of my bedroom where I had sought refuge from the world. "In My Room" was a song that had struck a special chord for me, and saying good-bye was like leaving an old friend. I took one last look at the memorabilia I had collected over the 18 years; the set of World Book Encyclopedias, pictures of Mickey Mantle and Al Kaline, my pitcher's glove and posters of Corvettes and dragsters, turned off the lights, then headed downstairs.

Come On All Of You Big Strong Men

When the time of departure arrived, my dad said, "Go say goodbye to your mother." She was taking my enlistment pretty hard, but it was a bittersweet moment. She was losing her son and yet she was probably relieved that my going would soothe the friction between my father and me.

I remember her eyes pooling with tears as I hugged her and said, "Don't worry, Mom, I'll be all right. Besides, it's not like I'm going to Vietnam. I'll be back for leave when I finish boot camp." She was not seeing me in my manhood, but the little boy with the combed blond hair and sad green eyes that day when she had taken me into her arms at the orphanage. Big boys didn't cry unless they were sissies, or so my father had stressed, so I bit my upper lip, swallowed back the tears and left.

3

Boot

My dad drove me downtown to the recruiter's office. It was festooned with slick posters of proud Marines in dress blues, soldiers looking more like male models than grunts, and Airmen and Sailors looking like they had chosen the ultimate career. It was a strained twenty-minute ride with a brooding silence hanging over us like a gray skyscape. When we pulled up in front of the Federal Building, a couple dozen teenagers were milling about or clustered in small pockets smoking cigarettes or fidgeting impatiently. Some were in a more jocular mood, while others savored their final moments of solitude, lounging on the steps or standing apart with a sullen, faraway expression on their faces.

I started to get out of the car, trying not to look my father in the eyes when he said, "You are going to be okay. Just do what they tell you." It was an uncomfortable moment for both of us. He shifted sideways in the seat and stuck out his hand. We shook, then I leaned over and kissed him on the cheek. There were no goodbyes.

I shut the door and headed up the steps of the Federal

Building to check out our 11:00 A.M. departure. The first thing I did was hit up a vending machine and purchased a pack of potent Pall Malls. It was the brand my father had smoked for thirty years. I was going to prove to myself that I was just as hard core as he was.

We were rounded up and loaded onto a bus for Detroit where we transferred to another bus which arrived at the gate of the Great Lakes Training Station about 2:00 A.M. in the morning. I remember being awakened by the hydraulic sound of the bus brakes and the throaty downshift of the diesel engine as we stopped at the entrance gate and were waved through by military policemen wearing white spats. The long ride had left me exhausted and disoriented—just the zombie-like condition designed by military training minds as the first stage of a well thought out program of dehumanization and loss of identity. It seemed like all green recruits arrived in the twilight-zonish hours of early morning, disgorged in a state of mental and physical fatigue into the waiting arms of drill sergeants who welcomed us with shouts and curses and taunts.

We were marched to some vintage barracks—circa World War II. I remember the musty odor of old wood, new paint, polishing compound and woolen blankets as we entered the barracks. Rows of double bunks and battleship gray lockers awaited us along each side of the bay. The opaque glare of naked bulbs suspended from the ceiling stung my bloodshot eyes as I blinked and tried to adjust to the light. Mercilessly, we were assigned bunks and told to get some sleep. Less than two hours later, we were sadistically rousted back to a semi-comatose state at 4:30 in the morning. The sky hadn't even begun to flush with pre-dawn grays.

It suddenly hit me that I wasn't at summer camp where I could go home if I got too homesick. I could just see myself tugging on the drill sergeant's sleeve and whining, "This is a real bummer, drill sergeant, I think I made a big mistake. Can I go home now?" Short of A.W.O.L., there was no way out. I was trapped, the victim of the system on my own. I had been reduced to a serial number, a lowly boot, a stinking maggot. Even Rod wasn't with me. He had gone to Tijuana, Mexico to revel in the flesh-pots before he went to boot camp, but he got so wasted on mescal and ten dollar prostitutes that he missed the bus by two weeks.

Over the next few days we shuffled like sleepwalkers through a catatonic state of physical and mental fatigue. We trudged from one processing station to the next undergoing the preliminary initiation rites into the service. At first we were herded around in our civies. We would see other groups of "out of place" looking adolescents in civilian clothes along with those dressed in dungarees and baby blue workshirts. We all felt helpless, uncoordinated and lost. It was all pre-planned.

We spent those first few days "hurrying to wait" in another line, standing in anxious rows waiting to get vaccinated by pimpley-faced corpsmen with pressurized syringes who looked like they'd take just as much delight in torturing cats or dismembering frogs. We were marched to an enormous supply building to get measured and fitted and assigned an inventory of clothing and gear from the top of our heads to the soles of our feet with Navy issue boxer shorts in between. We got our first taste of chow lines and mess halls and formations, and we experienced the ultimate degradation of our manhood at an assembly line barber shop which seemed more like a sheep shearing station in the Australian outback than a barber shop. Several quick strokes of the razor gave our heads the naked Buddhist monk look of stubby white skinheads.

We began to emerge from the initial daze and settle into the routines of boot camp when we were assigned a company commander. Ours was a real jewel—a throwback to prehistoric times. He was a reptilian-looking character, long and lizard-like with bulging eyes that blinked with irritating regularity. He was a confirmed lifer with faded tattoos on each forearm and the mouth of a sewer. He was one of those characters who bullies subordinates to compensate for their lack of leadership; a petty little men who reveled in his role as "lord of the boots" with the perverted arrogance of Captain Bly or the commandante of some banana republic. His vocabulary seemed to consist of only a couple hundred words, 90 percent of which were prefixed and suffixed with profane putdowns. We were slandered and called queers, pukes, squirrels, girls and obscene characterizations we had never heard of. He had the verbal finesse of a drunken sailor, which in fact, was his condition half the time.

When we were issued our clothing, we were ordered to stencil our names on everything so they wouldn't get lost in laundering. We then were ordered to bundle up our civilian clothing and mail them back to our parents along with a letter to mom and dad saying that everything was just great, we were having the time of our lives, and the drill instructors were some of the kindest, warmest, most caring individuals we had ever met. We didn't actually write the letters. They were already written for us. All we had to do was sign our name, like P.O.W.'s signing a propaganda confession prepared by their captors.

After about a week, we were transferred to barracks on the other side of the base. It served as the basic training compound. It really wasn't that rough though. Most of the horror stories of boot camp are melodramatic hype meant to intimidate moronic trainees. It was mostly just a big game. If you played by the rules, didn't mouth off, show too much initiative, or manifest more than a double digit I.Q., everything went just fine. There was always the daily ration of harassment and petty regulations, but for the most part it wasn't much different than a government sponsored summer camp.

In auditoriums and in the field, we were taught how to wash our clothes, arrange our lockers and stand seabag inspection. We were taught how to salute, march in formation and distinguish insignia and rank. We learned about being on a ship and how to swim. We did countless calisthenics, push-ups and obstacle courses. We learned how to clean and assemble a rifle, how to scrub urinals with toothbrushes, and how to spit polish our boots until you could see your face in the reflection. Some of us even discovered the hidden secrets of "Glow-Coat"—the forbidden shortcut to boot polishing. But above all, we learned the value of unity, of working with others, and how to follow orders. And everywhere we marched and marched and marched.

In our fifth week of boot camp we had to stand guard as part of our training. It included all the time honored rituals of challenging intruders, requesting the proper password and guarding some strategic location, like an abandoned warehouse, motorpool, or garbage cans in the dead of night with the seriousness of sentries guarding an ICBM silo. We were issued vintage M-1 rifles that looked like they'd last been used on Guadalcanal and assigned a prearranged groove to pace back and forth in for several lonely hours.

That's when it hit me. I had pulled one of the more prestigious assignments guarding dipsy dumpsters from 6:00 P.M. to 10:00, but I had to go to chow hall at 4:40 to eat before my watch. Early into my guard duty, I started cramping in my stomach. At first I thought it was gas or something from dinner. But when sharp pains jabbed into my stomach with such excruciating force that I nearly doubled over, I knew something was serious. Leaving your post during guard duty was a Court Martial offense so I stuck it out. I requested to see a doctor when I was relieved, but I was told that I was a big baby faking the pain to get out of work. This went on for several hours until I couldn't even stand up. My demands finally got me a trip to the dispensary at about four in the morning.

When a medic poked his forefinger in my side with the gentleness of an inquisitive gorilla, I nearly passed out. In five minutes I was in an ambulance with sirens blaring and red lights flashing on my way to Great Lakes Naval Hospital. Within an hour, I was prepped, administered anesthetic, and put under the scalpel for an emergency appendectomy to remove a ruptured appendix. I almost died.

My folks came to see me in the hospital a couple days later. It was a warm reunion. They seemed to be proud of me, that I was doing so well. I remember fantasizing about how much more glorious it would have been to have taken a bullet instead of a ruptured appendix, but it was satisfying to see their support none the less.

There were forty occupied beds on each side of the ward, but I was the only one of eighty men who was not a Vietnam casualty. Each of the stainless steel beds had an American flag draped at the foot of the frame. It was a moving memorial to see the patriotic symbol of Old Glory hanging in reverent reminder of brave young men who had poured out a sacred offering of blood upon the alter of sacrifice for their country.

The images of boy soldiers crippled and maimed, without arms and legs was emotionally overwhelming. Some looked like mummies with heads and stumps wrapped with thick layers of gauze. Some were tethered to I.V.'s or suspended by trapeze cables. Others showed no physical wound except for the telltale bedding lying strangely depressed where legs once had been. Many were in pain, but confronted it with a determined dignity void of any complaining or self-pity.

I could tell my father was having a hard time as he surveyed the sterilized carnage. Most of them were not even old enough to vote. They were just punk kids barely out of puberty. I remember the haunting echoes from the past in my mother's voice when she said, "Honey, look at them, they are the age you were when you went into the Army and left for New Guinea."

One of the patients was wearing a 1st Cavalry patch

from the same division my father had fought with through the jungles and swamps of the South Pacific. When my dad spotted the patch, he got up and headed over to his bedside. In moments, they looked like long lost buddies by the way they were getting along. At the time, it seemed odd that showing compassion to a total stranger seemed so natural, but I had not yet learned of the sacred bond and quiet camaraderie of men who have seen "the Elephant" and experienced the "baptism of fire."

After a few days of convalescence in the ward, I was discharged and assigned to a holding company. I tried to hitch a ride across the base with my seabag, but giving a ride to a lame trainee was as popular as picking up a leper. I was forced to walk, but the weight of my pregnant seabag ripped my sutures open.

I couldn't believe how callous and indifferent the system could be if you fell through the bureaucratic cracks. I was just a boot and ranked on the evolutionary scale alongside invertebrates like jellyfish and slugs. As a consequence, I was dumped in a disciplinary holding company of dereicts and misfits until my stitches healed. It was the dark side of "F-Troop" and "Hogans Heros." It reminded me more of a Bronx holding tank on Saturday night than anything remotely resembling boot camp. Some of them were processing out of the service with dishonorable discharges or waiting to be recycled through the system for one more try to reform them into model trainees. Most had just gotten released from the brig. It was a motley crew of druggies, A.W.O.L.'s, slackers, criminals and anti-authority types.

I was scared to death in that claustrophobic nut house. They had handmade shivs and crude weapons. I really feared that I was going to get jumped or stabbed. I felt like a stray mutt waiting to be gassed in the city pound. I kept asking myself, "What am I doing in this outfit? I'm just a clean cut kid from Grand Rapids, Michigan." I phoned my father and practically begged him to get me out of there. But he couldn't do much except to say, "You just hang in there, you won't get killed in boot camp. Go see the chaplain." But I didn't want to see the chaplain because he probably would think I was a wimp, so, I stuck it out, keeping my mouth shut, and trying not to stare at anyone for too long. After ten days on Devil's Island, the paperwork finally caught up with me. I was paroled back to another basic training company in the same week of training I had dropped out of. By chance, I ended up in the same company my buddy Rod was in. He had finally overcome his hangover and caught the bus to basic.

Because I had a two week jump in time and grade, I was appointed Master-of-Arms. As far as boots were concerned, I had ascended to the top of the pecking order. It was a real "kick back job." If someone got out of line, I came down on them. It was skate duty, which didn't win me any friends during the remaining weeks of basic.

4

Booze & Tattoos

After eight weeks, I had run the gauntlet of basic training and graduated with another mass produced company of cookie-cutter sailors. My parents came to the graduation ceremonies. It had all the traditional props: marching formation, brass bands, banners and company standards, well-worn speeches, and bleachers filled with beaming parents.

My orders were cut, giving me a two week leave before heading to the sprawling naval base at Norfolk, Virginia for fleet duty. They were two of the best weeks of my life. My dad bent over backwards to show me how proud he was. It was a look I had never seen in his eyes before. I had finally earned his respect and was no longer just a punk kid. He demonstrated his approval by handing me the keys to a new 1967 bronze XL Ford convertible. He said it was for me to use during my liberty. Gas was only 29.9, and a couple of bucks bought me a lot of cruising with the wind blowing through my fresh crop of hair. I spent those two weeks driving around like some war hero showing off to the girls, having a few beers with my buddies, listening to the Beach Boys and the Righteous Brothers.

When I arrived at Norfolk, I was assigned to the U.S.S. *NorthHampton*. It was a sophisticated communications and intelligence ship, which I didn't think was too intelligent. Assigning me to an intelligence ship made about as much sense as rearranging deck chairs on the *Titanic*. Again, the proverb was vindicated, "There's the right way, and the wrong way, and the Navy way."

I'll never forget my first impressions. I felt like a country hick seeing the big city for the first time. I had used the travel voucher the navy had given me to fly to Virginia, then caught a cab at the airport which drove right to the pier where the *NorthHampton* was moored. The hustle and bustle of the base, the briny smell of salt water, and the awesome sight of my ship were breathtaking. It was over four stories tall and looked to me like a towering gray Matterhorn. I remember looking up the gangplank and thinking, "How am I going to get me and my seabag way up there from way down here?" It was a struggle, but I pulled myself to the top a bit ruffled and out of breath, but happy that I was going to see the world at last.

Like every seaman apprentice before me, I soon got lost in the maze of corridors and stairwells in my attempts to locate my berthing compartment. My fellow shipmates took pretty good care of me. There were the traditional practical jokes like sending me to the paint locker to fetch a gallon of bulkhead remover or a yard of flightline, but all in all, they knew I was new onboard and kind of treated me like their kid brother.

A few days later, we set sail for our duty station in the Caribbean. I'll never forget the rush of exhilaration when I heard the guttural groan of the engines as they came to life deep within the bowels of the ship. I'll never forget the faint vibration from the massive screws, the casting off of lines, the goodbye waves from tearful young wives, and the glorious sense of adventure as the hull caressed the pier, then gently slipped away.

Our mission would take us down the eastern seaboard to Puerto Rico, St. Thomas and to Guantanamo Bay on the eastern tip of Cuba. Our job was to eavesdrop on Cuban communications with the Russians, monitor ship traffic and function in all the top secret realms of electronic surveillance.

It sounded exciting with overtures of James Bond, but that's where the adventure stopped for me. I was far removed from the cloak and dagger intrigue. I was just a lowly swabby assigned to the deckforce. It was the navy equivalent of ditch digger, wetback, and manual laborer. The romantic glitter of sea duty was torpedoed just after we cleared port. For the next six months I sweated and toiled through the navy's equivalent of a Georgia chain gang chipping paint, swabbing the deck, and painting oceans of red-lead primer.

The monotonous grind of sea duty, locked into an endless grind of mind-numbing routine, unable to escape from a floating island, drove men to an insatiable lust to do something exciting—anything to awaken senses dulled by relentless boredom.

Before I went into the service, I played it pretty straight. When my friends would be chugalugging six packs like thirst starved camels, I would sip a beer or two at the most. With my father's warden mentality, I didn't dare come home drunk. To do so would definitely have had an adverse affect on my mental and physical well-being. But my new found freedom and mounting frustration changed all of that. Out of my father's reach and mother's watchful eye, I quickly degenerated into a drunken libertine whose all-consuming passion was to party with the abandon of a reprobate.

The navy didn't help. It wasn't exactly a haven for churchgoers or temperance workers. Sloppy, gutter drunk caricatures of drunken sailors weren't invented in colorful imaginations, but in bars and brothels of a thousand ports of call. You weren't a real salt unless you could hold your booze and act like a real "swinging jock." I really wanted to play the role. Looking back, I can't believe how much fun it was to lay slumped in a toilet stall reeking of old urine, hugging a vomit splattered bowl with the desperation of a beaten prizefighter, wretching your guts out from the effects of cheap booze.

I experienced my initial descent into the raunchy world of fallen sailors in Old San Juan. It was a cesspool of wall to wall merchants whose sole ambition in life seemed to revolve around hustling sailors by pandering to their baser instincts. It was a festering sewer of sleazy bordellos, trashy tattoo parlors, and gaudy souvenir shops peddling obscene trinkets to lonely men with money to burn. It was also a haven for countless bars with back home names like "Bottoms Up," "The Chicago Club," and "Lucky Seven." They were filthy dives with loud rock music, sultry lights and hordes of streetwise prostitutes who cruised the strip with the predatorial instincts of circling sharks.

One of the more popular pastimes of sailors in port was to take the tour of the Bacardi rum factory in Puerto Rico. You did the tour like dutiful tourists, and graciously accepted the free samples of liquor with the feigned innocence of kindergarteners receiving chocolate milk samples on the dairy field trip. We scrounged all the free booze we could get our hands on, then we would down a fifth of whiskey, and a bottle of 150-proof rum with tequila chasers until we were totally annihilated. When we were well beyond the limits of being legally drunk, we'd grope our way into Old San Juan to raise hell.

One of the first things I did was to get a tattoo. You couldn't really claim to have gotten your "sea legs" until your arms had been stitched with a tattoo from some legendary place like Naples, Hong Kong, or San Juan. I remember stumbling into one especially nasty looking parlor whose walls were covered with garish tattoos of every description. There were cobras and skulls and barebreasted mermaids and hearts with "Love Mom" and Playboy rabbits and eagles and anchors and Madonnas. The tattoo artist looked like he came out of an old Humphrey Bogart movie. He was a piggish looking character with a dirty, sweat stained T-shirt, breath that would peel paint, and a three day growth of beard. He performed his craft hunched over you with a cigarette and an inch and a half of ashes dangling out of the corner of his mouth.

I had a buddy who got so knee-walking drunk on leave in Hong Kong that a couple of shipmates dragged him into the tattoo parlor, took off his shoes and socks, and paid the artist to tattoo "Made in Hong Kong" on the soles of his feet. Then they took a polaroid snapshot and mailed it back to his wife. But my first involvements with the seedy world of tattoo parlors was more conservative. I plopped down a few bucks and selected the initials "P.B.R." which stood for "Pabst Blue Ribbon" beer and a small American eagle. Unbeknownst to me at the time, it would take on a double meaning down the road. Twenty minutes under the sting of the electric needle, a couple dabs of dye, and I swaggered out sporting the proud mark of a beer guzzling juicer.

Several layers of youthful innocence were stripped away in one of the more infamous watering holes I frequented known as "The Texas Bar." It doubled as a bar and brothel with a raucous barroom downstairs and sleazy whorehouse upstairs. That's where I lost my virginity. The place was filled with tawdry looking prostitutes in skin tight mini skirts who were weathered veterans in the seductive arts of sauntering up to sailors and propositioning them for a few minutes of cheap thrills. The first time one of the girls came on to me, I felt like it was something I was obligated to do or I'd never live down the shame in the eyes of my more seasoned shipmates.

You paid your ten bucks and were handed a towel and a prophylactic and led upstairs to a dingy little booth. I was so nervous and embarrassed. I tried to act cool, but it was all over before I knew it. The whole attitude was, "hurry up and get this thing over with. I've got more customers waiting downstairs." When I finished, she pushed me off, slithered into her skirt and left, leaving me questioning, "This is what everybody is talking about?" I remember laying there staring at the peeling plastered ceiling feeling dirty and violated. The whole rotten experience was vulgar and repulsive. But I got up and buttoned up my pants and played the role. I walked downstairs like a thousand fallen youth before me and bragged about how fantastic it was. But inside, I think we all knew how very empty and unfulfilling it had been.

The Texas Bar was a place where a lot of pent-up frustration was released. There were usually several ships anchored in the harbor at any given time and there was a lot of inter-ship rivalry between the crews. This made for some very volatile situations when you added all the booze you could drink. I had my first barroom brawl at the Texas Bar. It was total chaos, like something out of an old west saloon fight—broken chairs, flying bottles, shattered glass. It was impossible to remain an innocent bystander. You had to fight just to survive. There was no "Marques of Queensbury" rules or gentlemanly courtesies in these fights. They were an "every man for himself, punch, bite, kick, gouge, thrash, knuckle-fisted free-for-all." That's where I learned the value of a cue stick. It was great for splintering across some poor slob's face. That brawl soon escalated into a riot between the Americans and Puerto Ricans, and spread like wildfire through Old San Juan. They had to finally call out the National Guard to subdue it. The Shore Patrol was splitting heads with billy clubs, and rounding up sailors by the dozens and throwing them into the brig. But somehow, I managed to make it back to my ship unscathed.

After a few shore leaves, whoring and drinking and brawling came easy. I even grew to like it. There would be times I could barely hold myself up to the bar when I'd notice some guy whose face I didn't like, and I would just walk up and cram a beer bottle between his eyes. It hadn't taken long, but as far as the human condition was concerned, I had deteriorated to the level of bilge water by the end of my first six months of fleet duty.

5

"The Best Laid Plans . . ."

After six months of fleet duty, I had reached the limits of my tolerance. It wasn't that I had had my fill of partying from one port to the next, heaving my guts out from an overdose of beer, or nursing bruised battlewounds from barroom brawls. I was far from any prodigal coming to his senses in the sour slop of a pig pen. It was the everlasting chipping and scraping and sanding and polishing and painting and swabbing. I was fed up with being a maritime janitor.

I had climbed a couple rungs in rank and grade and enjoyed the sense of responsibility it conferred, but I didn't want to be enslaved on the *NorthHampton*'s deck force for the rest of my enlistment. Three and a half more years of drudgery had about as much appeal to me as being exiled to a Siberian labor camp.

It was at the height of my frustration that I met Michelle. We were back in port at Norfolk at the time. I bumped into her at the Christian Servicemen's Home. It was an outreach organized by a church group to offer social activity to lonely servicemen—something akin to the

U.S.O. I wasn't much into donuts, coffee, or the Lawrence Welk atmosphere of those gatherings, but it was a great place to crash on weekends. Michelle was from my neck of the woods in Lansing, Illinois and had volunteered to do some summer outreach work in the Norfolk tidewater area.

My first impressions of her caught me off guard with the same force of an unsuspecting cue stick in a bar brawl. She was absolutely stunning. Compared to the coarse vulgarity of San Juan prostitutes with their loud makeup and louder mouths, Michelle was as different as night and day. She was a shapely, long-legged beauty with silken texture skin, azure blue eyes, and alluring curves which accentuated her model-like frame. She was a captivating beauty with an almost subtle sensuousness tempered only by a purity of spirit. There was nothing artificial in her sensuousness. With Michelle it came naturally.

But the magnetism I felt came from more than the contrast between her wholesome beauty and the wayward wantonness of Caribbean whores. The contrast between ourselves was also as different as light and darkness. She was naive and undefiled. I was worldly wise. She was virtuous, clean cut and moral, while my fiber had been twisted and gnarled by my escapades to the south.

Suffice to say, I fell head over heels for her and found myself craving her winsome beauty with the fervency of a terminally ill patient who will sacrifice anything and everything to possess the last remaining dose of medicine to cure his disease. I was heartstruck and sick for her affections. I struggled to play it cool with the slightest trace of feigned ambivalence, but I was about as restrained in the mating ritual as a dog in heat. I had dated girls in high school and even flirted with puppy love, but the chemistry between us was more volatile than adolescent infatuation.

The attraction was mutual. I was not some love struck sailor destined to pine away from the ill effects of unrequited love. She had never met anyone like me. I was everything her parents hoped and prayed she wouldn't meet, let alone fall in love with. Her parents had shielded her from anyone remotely resembling my character with the protectiveness of the secret service. But now she was alone and vulnerable, and free to explore the womanly passions which revolted against her youthful innocence. I'm sure she was attracted to me with the same perverse curiosity of a moth drawn to the flame. I was rebellious and coarse and everything she was forbidden to touch. Maybe that's why we were drawn to each other with such compelling force. I wanted her because she was untouched. She wanted me because I was forbidden. I'm sure she could sense the danger, but there is an intoxicating perversity in temptation. It is an almost irresistible dare that solicits and charms and seduces before it finally destroys. It's the "spider and the fly," the cheese in the trap, the sign whose "off limits" subtly beckons. I was the serpent lurking in her Eden.

We spent a passionate summer, grasping for stray moments together, oblivious to time and space. We were lost to each other in reckless abandon. Michelle and I seemed to cling to each other with an unspoken desperation, as if we both sensed ominous forces which threatened to wrench us apart. As if to forestall the inevitable separation when she returned to Grand Rapids to attend Calvin College in the fall, we got engaged. In our last fleeting moments we made our Polyanna plans for the future. She would finish her schooling. I would complete my enlistment; then return to live with Michelle happily ever after.

When the time came, neither of us wanted to part. We had pledged ourselves to each other forever, but I secretly feared that unless I could find some way to be close to her, our relationship would eventually unravel. I had given her just enough taste of the world to whet her appetite for more. I was the "pusher" and she was my junkie, who might soon seek out another if I couldn't supply her habit. But there didn't seem to be any way out of our dilemma.

The navy had me by the throat and short of A.W.O.L., I was at their mercy.

I wracked my brains for days trying to figure out a way to get back to Michelle, when finally it dawned on me. When the answer came, it seemed so simple that I was surprised I hadn't stumbled onto it earlier. It was like something clicked inside, like all the gears were lining up at the same time. Great Lakes Naval Hospital was the answer. It was within driving distance of Grand Rapids and if I could worm a transfer I could at least see Michelle on the weekends.

There was only one catch. I would have to volunteer to become a medic and attend the corpsmen training course. With my past performance in school, I was worried that my application would be rejected. But my concerns were premature. My previous exposure to corpsmen was limited to the sanitized routine of orderlies on the ward where I had my appendix out. I knew it would involve some disagreeable duties like changing fouled bed pans, and disposing soiled bandages or spoon feeding amputees, but if it would get me closer to Michelle it was a sacrifice I was willing to make.

What I didn't know was how willing the navy was to accept applications. The navy was only the front door to much grimmer realities. Everything seemed harmless enough on the outside, but it was as deceptive as the "Bates" motel. The navy served as a conduit to funnel conscientious objectors and selfless humanitarians into front line duty in 'Nam, tending to wounded and dying Marines. Even worse, their casualty rate was appalling. Along with M-60 gunners, radio men and forward observers, not to mention an endless stream of green 2nd Lieutenants, medics had one of the highest kill ratios. I was destined to spend several naive weeks chuckling to myself how glad I was that I wasn't in the Marines. But the navy had the last laugh. When I signed the medic application forms at Norfolk, I failed to note the rueful grin on the clerk's face. I was oblivious to the fact that I was signing my life away.

At first, everything went according to plan. I got the transfer to Great Lakes and tackled my courses with a renewed enthusiasm to succeed, encouraged by my week-end rendevous with Michelle and newfound desire to re-form my ways. I enjoyed an extra measure of respect from my classmates because I was an "old salt" in their eyes. Most of them were fresh out of boot camp while I had gotten my sea legs in fleet duty, and even had a tattoo from San Juan.

In spite of my newfound stability, the timing had an ironic twist. Great Lakes had become a political hotbed in the midst of growing instability and social unrest. By the summer of '67 America was seized in the thrawldoms of anti-war sentiment. The weekly casualty count was es-calating in Southeast Asia and graphic six o'clock footage of frenzied firefights and bloodied soldiers was bringing closer to home the distant reality that American boys were dying. It was no longer just a rumor of war.

In spite of McNamara's claims and Westmoreland's glowing assurances of certain victory, a growing majority was sensing that we were locked in a bloody war of attri-tion without territorial objectives whose primary goal seemed to be proportional body counts and kill ratios. Political dissent, student riots, and peace marches con-verged with the turbulent cultural cross currents of the late '60s to encourage a steady erosion of national support for a war which was increasingly perceived as immoral and unjust.

It was the season of Watts and Newark and the Black Panthers, Berkeley and Cambridge and San Francisco State, General Hershey and the draft, S.D.S., pacifists and the Chicago Seven, Flower Children, Sergeant Pepper, "The Summer of Love," and 'Nam. It was a time of war, and calls for peace, and a time of national confusion on all fronts. From college campuses to the Halls of Congress, from students to housewives, it became increasingly popular to distance yourself from the war and those who were fighting it. It mattered not what the motive or how noble the intent. Men and women in uniform were caught in a no-man's-land between the hard line hawks and so-called doves. We were stigmatized by society and scorned as social morons and mindless misfits for wearing a uniform.

Men who, just forty-eight hours earlier, had been crossing fields of fire through a muddy rice paddy or humping through a hostile jungle were spit on and greeted with taunts of "Baby Butcher" and "Murderer" when they stepped off their plane, and for the first time encountered the full brunt of national contempt.

But those who languished in the wards at Great Lakes seemed to me to have been wounded the worst by the scorn. Some took it in stride; others could not. The pain in their eyes went deeper than torn nerves and shattered bones. They wore forever saddened faces—the beaten, burdened expressions of men betrayed.

But even for those of us who had not yet gone, the contempt was no less galling. Many of our peers, sometimes even our best friends, began to view the military and all associated with it as symbols of a war which was despised by a growing chorus of Americans.

In my six month absence, epic changes had altered the course of American opinion. I returned to witness firsthand just how close the dissension had come to home. Great Lakes Naval Training Center was sandwiched halfway between the University of Chicago and the University of Wisconsin in Madison. So we found ourselves under siege, deluged by zealous busloads of anti-war protesters with the clockwork regularity of Disneyland tours.

They were a mixed bunch of mangy midwest hippies, campus radicals, cause conscious students, and politically active citizens who came to march by the hundreds and sometimes thousands outside the gates, shaking angry clenched fists at fidgeting young guards or flashing the peace sign in a shallow show of universal brotherhood.

They came with banners reading, "Down with Fascist Aggression," "Stop the Draft," "Thou Shalt Not Kill," "Make Love Not War," and "Peace Now!" Some contemptuously waved Viet Cong flags while others burned ours in effigy or trampled it underfoot like so much garbage. At times they shuffled back and forth in Ghandi-like silence. At other times they marched in boisterous defiance shouting slogans like, "Hell, no we won't go," or "I don't give a damn for Uncle Sam. I'm not going to Vietnam!"

The ever-present camera crews always showed, with the inevitability of flies on a hog, filming and interviewing with the journalist neutrality of *Pravda*. No matter how they shot it and edited it and packaged it, we came out smelling as bad as an outhouse in August. It made for an impossible dilemma for young soldiers caught in the crossfire of national dissent. Our peers were saying one thing while our notions of patriotism dictated another.

I remember thinking, "Hey, what is this? This isn't the way it was in WWII. What would Sergeant Striker think? What about 'The Sands of Iwo Jima,' 'The Best Years of Our Lives,' and 'The Pride of the Marines'?" A uniform used to be something you were proud to wear. A guy in uniform could always get a free cup of coffee or a hitchhike anywhere. But things had changed. America had lost her way. And yet, in spite of all the verbiage on the evils of war, few really understood. They were just too far removed. It was easy for both sides, sheltered back in the safe confines of fortress America, to extol the virtues of patriotism and the American way. It was easy for weekend hippies and spoiled college kids with S-2 deferments to denounce American aggression. It was even easier for the ostrich-like masses of mainstream Americans to ignore Vietnam altogether. They could flick the channel or turn the page or turn off the radio. They could bury their heads in the sand and ignore it altogether if it got too uncomfortable. But only those who actually sacrificed a season of their lives in 'Nam understood the depths of its realities.

When I returned from 'Nam, I found it a paradox that people wouldn't believe me. I had tasted it and breathed it and lived it but it didn't register. The few that had an ear to hear what had happened couldn't bare the stories. They would respond with, "This is too much, I can't handle this," or they would half jokingly reply, "Mic, you've got to be the world's greatest liar."

It was like my months in 'Nam were held in limbo. Years later I'd try to describe what it was like to my wife, but she just couldn't find it in herself to believe me. She assumed I was just twigged out because I'd popped too many drugs or been hit too many times in bars. It wasn't until we attended a wedding of one of the guys I served with and we started reminiscing about Vietnam that she realized I had been telling the truth after all. He was saying the same things I was. We were speaking the same language—one that was foreign and incomprehensible to outsiders.

It was so easy for sidewalk protesters and armchair commentators to label us "baby butchers" or to characterize us as pyromaniac teenagers who giggled with psychotic delight at the mere thought of torching an innocent Vietnamese village with their zippo lighters. But they knew nothing of peasant farmers who plowed their rice paddies by day in time honored fashion behind a plodding water buffalo and stalked the jungles at night setting homemade booby traps which would maim and kill unsuspecting marines in the morning. They knew nothing of delicate young women who would walk up to you with a basket of eggs and a live grenade, or little runny nosed kids with a satchel charge strapped to their backs who would come begging a squad of G.I.'s for cigarettes or candy before blowing themselves up. But those back home knew next to nothing of these things. The six o'clock news rarely reported the whole truth, especially if it wasn't politically expedient.

In spite of all the Marxist clichés and utopian promises of a worker's paradise, naive idealists knew nothing of communism in Southeast Asia. To them, the Viet Cong were selfless revolutionaries seeking only to throw off the yokes of capitalistic tyranny. The Jane Fondas and Tom Haydens and self-styled champions of the "peace loving peoples" had no concept of the raw realities of communist ideology in Vietnam or the extent they would go to further their goals. Peel away the colorful banners and self-serving propaganda, and you witness the naked brutality of communism. You see it in all its ruthless barbarity. We saw it with gut-puking reality.

At the heart of their strategy was not noble speeches or acts of human kindness, but murder and coercion and crimson cruelty. The South Vietnamese peasants cared less whether we had come to liberate them from the red peril or the communists had come to free them from imperialistic aggression.

But what the villagers wanted was of no concern to the Viet Cong. They had other designs. They would enter a village not to pacify but to subdue. They were usually peaceful little enclaves consisting of private gardens, stray dogs, chickens, rooting pigs, and a score of simple hooches constructed of bamboo and thatch. They were dirt-poor settlements of illiterate rice farmers in black pajamas and conical hats, betelnut stained mama-sans, and half-clad children who just wanted to be left to themselves and their ancient rhythms.

A Viet Cong officer would herd the peasants into the center of the village and select one family to serve as an object lesson. The family's children would be lined up from the youngest to the eldest and a twelve to fourteen year old boy or girl would be chosen to serve as a human booby trap to carry a satchel charge to explode among unsuspecting G.I.'s. If the parents protested they would take the remaining brothers and sisters and hack off their arms with machetes and stack them in a pile in front of the villagers. They would then make all the other parents march around the mutilated children screaming in agony as they bled to death, until the object lesson sunk in. Such were the terror tactics of the Viet Cong. That's how they "won" over the people.

When they overran the city of Hue during the Tet offensive, they systematically tortured, butchered and disemboweled over 3,000 people. Many were even buried alive. But you heard next to nothing of this in the American press. They didn't want to print Viet Cong atrocities, they only wanted to play up ours. They only seemed to have a stomach for half-truths.

When we came home and tried to share the painful experiences with an old high school buddy over a beer, they couldn't take it. The nightmares and atrocities weighed so heavily on your mind, you needed someone to talk to just so you could get it off your chest. But no one wanted to hear, so you buried it and repressed it and burned your memories like a witch at the stake. And all the while you knew that no one understood what it was really like, except you and those who had lived it.

Even before I went to 'Nam, I faced a growing dilemma. Patriotic convictions prevented me from protesting the war. On the other hand, I had no desire to go to Vietnam and risk coming home in a box. And every day I worked the wards and viewed firsthand the grim aftermath of war. Come to think of it, I didn't have much of a stomach for death and dying either. I was no more conditioned to it than the sheltered mindset of America who was used to viewing the sanitized versions of war at a safe distance. Maybe that's why, when confronted with the technicolor brutality, human nature revolts and denys and avoids the truth.

So, I found myself escaping, anything to get away from the suffering on the wards or protesters prowling the gates.

It was a dreamscape of painful images. Nineteen year old marines would be lying on the ward with multiple stumps where healthy limbs had been a few weeks earlier. They were my age. Their lives were shattered. They would lay in their beds with sad luminous eyes contemplating a life of handicaps, pain, Veteran's hospitals, and disability checks. Still, most of them lay there courageously trying to salvage something out of their broken manhood. They endured the pain and fought back the tears. I had my own pain, but it was nothing compared to those guys.

Eight hours a day on the ward was about all I could handle. When my hospital shift knocked off at four o'clock, I headed for our local hangout called the "Rathskeller." It was like an oasis in the midst of a desert. It was a place to breathe again, to forget, to dull the images of suffering. Looking back, it was a place of blunted realities—more like a mirage than a sanctuary of forgetfulness. It was our place to numb out to pitchers of beer and sentimental tunes from the juke box. There was one by the Boxtops whose lyrics affect me even to this day:

> *"Got to get a ticket for a fast plane*
> *ain't got time for a fast train*
> *Lonely days are goin'*
> *I'm a goin' home*
> *My baby she wrote me a letter . . .*
> *She wrote me a letter said*
> *She couldn't live without me comin' home"*

It spoke of times when Michelle and I would be together.

My duties on the ward consisted of changing beds and bedpans, giving injections, changing bandages, and assisting doctors on their rounds when they removed dressings or cleaned sutures, and generally trying to make the men as comfortable as possible. The antiseptic smells of surgical rubber, sterile soaps, medication, and fresh sheets mingled with the faint pungent odor of body fluids, old blood, and stained bandages. They were the smells of wounded men—a constant reminder of sufferings past and present and yet to come. The atmosphere on the wards was sometimes depressing, though doctors, orderlies, and nurses struggled to maintain an air of professionalism and cheerful optimism, even in the face of heartbreaking tragedy.

Eighty stainless steel beds wrapped in crisp white sheets lay in formation along each side of the ward. Many were rigged with additional configurations of bars and cables and pulleys for patients in various postures of traction. At the front of each bed were two American flags; one more than when I had been on the ward with appendicitis.

Maybe in some small way it was an additional patriotic gesture to compensate for the opposition outside the gates. Men who had not yet turned twenty lay prostrate before two symbolic pieces of cloth honoring their sacrifices. They were a mute, almost insignificant token of respect when compared to the price they had paid—160 flags commemorating missing arms and legs, crippled bodies in traction, bloodstained sheets, yellowed gauze, tormented groans and sweat-soaked night screams of boy-soldiers who had lost their youth before its time.

Sometimes the suffering was overwhelming, even at a distance. The condition of a couple of patients I routinely attended was particularly unnerving. One guy had been shredded by shrapnel. Another trooper in front of him snagged the trip wire and took the full force of the blast while the guy I was attending was sprayed with a red-hot sheet of shrapnel in the back blast. That's one of the vicious realities of shrapnel. It is totally indiscriminate and unpredictable. Sometimes there's not enough left of a man to put in a band-aid box; at other times a tiny razor-sharp sliver no bigger than a pin head can find its way to the heart or head with lethal results.

The trooper had been on patrol with the 1st Cavalry

Division when he was hit. His body was pockmarked with gouges. The shrapnel from the blast had torn fist-sized chunks of flesh from his calves and thighs and blown away his knee cap; his legs and buttocks looked like raw hamburger. Some of the wounds were open and draining and so deep you could see the bone.

Cleaning his raw flesh must have been excruciatingly painful, but he seldom winced or cried out. He would just grit his teeth and take it. They would pump these guys full of morphine and demerol, but when you're touching exposed nerves and tendons and oozing flesh, there's only so much edge you can take off the pain. Yet he was so tough. I remember wiping his wounds with antiseptic solution nearly on the verge of tears and saying, "man if this was happening to me, I would be screaming my bloody head off."

I stumbled over myself apologizing; "I'm sorry, man, I'm sorry. I don't want to hurt you." And all he would say was, "Hey, don't worry about it, kid." That really floored me. He called me "kid" like it was an established fact, and I was older than he was. But it wasn't forced or condescending. It wasn't the march of years which had etched the premature furrows on his face, but grueling months of pressure in the killing zone. He'd earned the right to call me kid. He probably could have called a forty-year-old "kid" with just as much conviction. The guy hadn't even turned nineteen, hadn't even voted, probably never even balanced a checkbook or known a woman, and yet he was talking like an old man.

But the worst case was a blind, triple amputee. His parents had signed for him to join the marines when he was seventeen. He had married his high school sweetheart before he left for 'Nam, and now what was left of him was back, blind with an arm and both legs missing. He was eighteen, married to a seventeen year old wife and destined to spend the rest of his life wasting away in a wheelchair or on some forsaken amputee ward in a V.A.

hospital. It was all I could do from breaking into tears every time she came up to see him. She was just a frail little thing with sad teary eyes and the lost look of a stray puppy. She'd just sit by his bedside looking fearful and abandoned. It was daily scenes of suffering such as these that forced me to deny the heartache and callous my emotions lest they destroy me. I think the only thing that helped me maintain my sanity were my weekends with Michelle, the refuge of the Rathskeller, and a determination to concentrate on my medical classes.

My hard work as a student hospital corpsman was paying off. I progressed through my corpsman training with flying colors. My initial euphoria about being a navy corpsman had turned to profound gratitude working on the wards mostly among wounded marines. One thing I soon learned was that combat medics were given no special exemptions from bullet wounds or booby traps. The fact that they were messengers of mercy whose mission was to save life instead of taking it was inconsequential. It made no difference to a Viet Cong sniper if he knowingly blew the brains out of some medic who was responding to a desperate call for "corpsman" to save a fellow marine who was sprawled face down in the mud. The V.C. cared nothing about the rules of the Geneva Convention or the sacred covenant of mercy to sacrifice life and limb to reach a wounded marine even if it cost him his own life in attempting to save another's.

About three weeks from the completion of our training, a keen sense of anticipation began to filter through the students. We all knew that orders would be cut at graduation, assigning us to our duty stations. And we all knew that most would go to fill the ever depleted ranks of badly needed corpsmen serving the grunts in 'Nam. The anticipation was contagious even though I had convinced myself that I wasn't going to 'Nam, let alone any front line company. I just kept reminding myself, "Man, am I glad

I am learning how to be a hospital orderly and I'm not going with the marines."

When the anticipated day arrived to receive our orders, we were taken into a room to wait for the company commander. The biting scent of nervous sweat underscored the silence. In a few moments, the company commander entered with a clipboard and started prefunctorily reading off the names and their corresponding assignments. You could almost hear the drum roll as he repeated "Republic of Vietnam" after each name. The words sounded more like clods of dirt falling on a coffin than a simple notification.

Listening to the rollcall was like listening to a broken record. I remember the strange mesmerized state I was in as he called off the names followed by the repetitious "Fleet Marine School." The title was synonymous with Vietnam. My mind kept flashing back to the crippled marines on the ward and wondering how many in the room would end up like them. That's when I heard my name: "Block, Michael—Republic of Vietnam." I couldn't believe what I had heard. I wanted to call out, "What did you say?" but it was too late. The bell had tolled for me. I felt like the doctor had just asked me to be seated and said, "I don't quite know how to tell you this, Mr. Block. It never gets easier. I'm sorry, but you only have a few months left to live." Receiving orders for 'Nam was like receiving a death sentence.

That which I had feared most had come upon me. All my scheming and manipulating and dreaming about me and Michelle and our gumdrop heaven came crashing down around me. My carefully crafted plans had collapsed, vindicating the words immortalized by Steinbeck.

I remember feeling like a mule had kicked me in the stomach. I was defeated, nauseated, desperate. I plodded back to my barracks in a state of shock. "What was I going to do now? What about Michelle and happily ever after?''

That night I paced the half-lit barracks smoking cigarettes like a convict on death row, wondering whether the chaplain or a last minute reprieve from the governor would come first.

6

Green Faced Frogmen

I plodded ponderously across the base, lost in thought, before entering a smoking lounge. Except for a few chairs, a vinyl couch and a low coffee table with some magazines and newspapers scattered on top, it was empty. I slumped into the couch in total resignation to my fate, when I noticed a stack of *Stars and Stripes* laying on the table. I picked up one and thumbed through the pages somewhat indifferently; then flung it onto the stack of newspapers. I reached for another copy and was instantly struck by the cover photo. There were several commandos clad in tiger fatigues in small assault skiffs with their faces painted with green camouflage grease sticks. The caption seemed to jump off the page: "Navy Commandos in Vietnam."

That's when something clicked inside. There was no way of getting out of going to 'Nam, and taking off for Canada was out of the question, but at least I could go prepared. If I was going to get a round trip ticket to the armpit with only the first leg guaranteed, then I wanted to go with the meanest, baddest, most highly trained outfit in the world.

There was no way I was going to 'Nam ill-prepared. Six weeks of boot camp and a couple of months of advanced training gave teenagers about as much preparation for the rigors of 'Nam as kindergarten did in equipping you for college. It wasn't that the training was so anemic, but no amount of simulated warfare comes close to the real thing. When all was said and done, mock Vietnamese villages, live-fire obstacle courses, camouflaged uniforms, and blanks always left you knowing that the props and special effects were make-believe. Few took their training seriously. They were still playing army, only now the toys were larger and the sound effects more realistic. They were still shooting pop-up targets with the same childlike playfulness of neighborhood kids simulating "Bang, you're dead" war games.

Many would soon encounter the sobering realities of 'Nam. They were not going to fight innocent street battles where you could contest whether you were dead or not. Bullets and booby traps were real and young men were not immortal after all. They wouldn't be fighting neighborhood rivals but seasoned Viet Cong who had been fighting for generations. Before us had been the Cambodians, Japanese, and the French. They were old to the ways of jungle warfare. They could live off the land, improvise, and subsist on a handful of cold rice. We were stepping into a world where life had become one of the lowest commodities on the market. We would be up against dedicated fighters who were only too willing to sacrifice their life for the greater good. But, I had no intention of becoming a statistic. I just wanted to do my 12 months and catch the "Freedom Bird" home.

The following morning, I went to my company commander to request my second transfer. I entered his office, saluted and said, "Corpsman, Mickey Block, Sir." "What is it, Block?" he responded. "Sir, I don't really think I'm the 'guts and glory' type. I don't really think I'm Marine Corpsman material." In my mind I was no Audie Murphy or Sergeant York. He glanced at my folder for a few moments, then looked up and said, "Well, Block, Uncle Sam has dumped a lot of good money into your training. Don't you think you owe us something? What do you propose we do with you? I can't just change assignments every time some trainee doesn't like what he's doing. Can I?" "No sir, but I came across this article in *Stars and Stripes* about being a Special Forces Navy Commando and I think it's right up my alley."

His jaw dropped in surprise. He didn't expect my proposition. With a sardonic smile he shook his head and said, "Block, with all the hell raising you get into off base on weekends, I think you may be right." In a few minutes the change of orders were typed, signed, and I was sent home for a thirty-day leave.

Michelle and I spent every moment together. But there was an unspoken strain lurking beneath the surface. Almost by instinct, I was subtly distancing myself from her affections. In my own awkward way, I was trying to emotionally prepare her for the long separation which would take me half a world away. I was giving her a way out.

But looking back, I think I was testing her commitment to me. It would take genuine love for her affection to weather the long night of 'Nam.

There would be some intimate moments alone listening to melancholy songs whose lyrics would follow you for a lifetime, and I would talk to her about calling off our engagement. I had introduced her to the world but she was still so innocent and naive. She would just sit there looking half-girl, half-woman. Her hands would be folded in her lap and her eyes glistening with tears. They would roll down her cheeks and she'd whimper in a wounded voice, "Why, Mickey, did I do something wrong?" I'd try to tell her "No" and explain that I would be gone for a long time. I might not come back. I might not come back in one piece. It was better if she faced up to the possibilities now. I just wanted her to be sure. But she was a woman with deep emotions. She didn't want to hear of logic and reason.

I was giving her a way out, but inside I was hoping she wouldn't take it. I was always trying to act macho and in control of our relationship, but if the truth were known, I needed her far more than she needed me.

But she'd assure me, "It doesn't make any difference if you lose an arm or a leg. I'd still love you. I just love you for what you are, who you are." She'd hold her ground with the tenacity of a bulldog. She was convinced that I would be the only man she would ever love—could ever love.

As the days passed and my departure neared, I grew more and more nervous. Saying goodbye to Michelle was killing me inside; maybe because I desperately feared it would be the last. I couldn't bear the thought that she wouldn't be there when I got back. I was subconsciously preparing myself for the worst, even though she seemed to have no second thoughts.

As a defense mechanism, I found myself slowly shutting her out of my life. I would go for long walks by myself, or I would leave her with my parents while I cruised around aimlessly, chain-smoking cigarettes and trying to drown out my thoughts with the radio. I could tell by the hurt on her face that she sensed I was dumping her. She had given herself to me and now I was rejecting her.

Toward the end of my leave she started crying and pleaded, "Why are you acting like this? Don't you love me? Mickey, you don't even act like you want me around any more." I'd deny it, half selfishly swearing that I just didn't want her to get hurt. But I was struggling to guard my emotions more than hers.

When the day came for me to catch my flight to San Diego, I dressed in my starched dress whites, packed my seabag and drove Michelle to her girlfriend's house. She had stayed with my parents for the last couple of weeks, but she would be rooming with a schoolmate during her sophomore year. When I got back we planned to get married and get a small apartment. I tried to maintain as we embraced and said our goodbyes. She promised she d wait for me and gave me one last, longing kiss before I got into the car. I told her not to worry, that I'd be back. She said, "I love you, Mickey" with quivering lips and tear-stained cheeks. I said, "I love you, too, Michelle," choked back the tears, then drove off, stealing one last glance at her receding figure in the rear-view mirror.

I stopped back at my parents' house to say goodbye to the family. The atmosphere was very somber, very subdued. It wasn't like I was going to boot camp or Norfolk. We said our stoical goodbyes and left it there.

The atmosphere in the car was tense and uncomfortable, as my father drove me to the airport. Both of us were stiff and stilted, cautiously avoiding any mention of Vietnam. The few words which were exchanged had an artificial air about them—just superficial talk.

After my check-in at the ticket counter, we headed for a coffee shop to kill time before my plane arrived. I could tell the tension was taking its toll on my father. He was nervously squirming in his seat and looking around the lounge while he chain-smoked Pall Malls. His hands were trembling as he sipped his coffee—giving the appearance of a chronic worrier. The clock on the wall seemed to have crawled to a stop as we waited for my boarding announcement.

Awkward minutes passed in silence before he mustered enough control to say, "You know our physician, Dr. Carrol, he's been in the Naval Reserves for years. He checked out that outfit you're going into and said it shouldn't be too rough on you." You would have thought Charlton Heston had brought the assessment straight from Mt. Sinai. But what did the Naval Reserves know about jungle warfare. He was about as much of an authority on war as my high school buddies.

It was like saying, "Now just keep your head down, stay out of the line of fire, do what they tell you, and you'll be okay." It was an unconvincing attempt to reassure me and probably himself. But he knew it was going to be a lot tougher than either of us were willing to admit. His clumsy encouragement had the same hollow ring as telling someone, "Cheer up. Things are going to get better," even though you know they're going to get much worse.

When the boarding announcement came over the loud speaker, we headed to the ticket check-in counter. After an attendant checked my ticket and assigned me my seat, I turned to my father and said, "Well, looks like this is it." He knew that I knew there were things that should have been said, but for whatever inadequacies between us, they never would. "Just keep your head down like I said and you'll be okay." I screwed my face and pursed my lips in an awkward smile and said, "Yea, I will." There were no kisses, no embraces. We just shook hands in a restrained, businesslike manner, then I headed down the boarding ramp without looking back.

I landed at LAX and caught a connecting flight to San Diego Naval Base where my orders were processed. Upon arrival, I was promptly assigned to the Naval Amphibious Training Base on Coronado Island off the coast of Southern California. Coronado was the site of the Special Warfare Operations Training Center where the elite Navy SEALS began their rigorous training. SEALS was an acronym for "Sea, Air, and Land Special Forces."

If the marines were "looking for a few good men," the SEALS were looking for a few "weird" men. The standard joke in the Special Forces maintained that you had to have flunked the psychological exam at least twice to gain entrance. There was something slightly warped in the psychological profile which qualified them uniquely for the SEALS. You couldn't always detect it up front, but 'Nam served as a perfect seedbed to germinate the unique brand of insanity that lay dormant beneath the surface.

Years later, when I was majoring in psychology, I came across a humorous illustration which reminded me of my estimation of the SEALS.

A motorist was driving on an isolated road late at night when he suddenly has a blow out. He pulls over to the shoulder next to a ditch and gets out to change the tire. When he's getting the spare out of the trunk he notices a chain-link fence on the other side of the ditch and is shocked to see two hands clutching the wires. Someone is staring at him through the fence.

He rolls the tire to the front of the car and notices a sign in the headlights. He's parked next to a state mental hospital. He jacks up the car, unscrews the five nuts, and places them in the upturned hubcap. He removes the tire under the watchful glare of the stranger. The motorist is getting nervous from the stares. "What is a maniac doing loose at night? Why is he staring at me like that?"

The driver starts to roll the flat to the trunk when he accidently steps on the hubcap, flipping the nuts into the ditch. He crawls around groping for the nuts in the darkness. He only finds one. In a calm, collected voice, the mental patient says, "If you take a nut off each of the other wheels, put them on the fourth wheel, four nuts each, you'll get to a gas station." The motorist is dumbfounded. "Hey, that'll work! That's brilliant! What in the world are you doing here?" With that the patient replies, "I'm in here for being crazy; not stupid!"

The oft told story which seemed to make the rounds of the psych department each semester seemed to parallel my experiences with the SEALS. Candidates weren't stupid. In fact, many were extremely intelligent. But it always seemed that they had their share of crazies who were institutional material in their own peculiar way.

They were all tough—not only physically but mentally. They were aggressive and determined and hungry to prove they could go beyond the normal limitations of human endurance. Our SEAL instructors were adept at recycling and remolding these men into lean, mean, fighting machines.

At the time, the SEALS were an exclusive naval unit within the Special Forces with little public name recognition. Unlike the army's Green Berets, who had been glamorized by John Wayne and "The Green Berets," or patriotic lyrics like "fighting soldiers from the sky, fearless men who jump and die," the navy spent little in the way of public relations to romanticize the SEALS.

The first phase of Special Warfare training at Coronado was a conditioning period stressing physical exertion. It was nothing short of torturous. At times it bordered upon the sadistic, even trespassing the boundary occasionally. When we arrived, our cute little white sailor hats and sailor suits were taken away. We were issued Marine Corps covers, fatigues and combat boots. Gone were the leisurely days of basic training.

We were hustled out onto a large asphalt parking lot sadistically referred to as the "grinder," and ordered to stand at attention. I remember the intensity of the sun stinging my olive drab shoulders as we waited in formation. Wavering heat vapors rising from the blacktop served as a dreaded portent of our coming initiation into purgatory. That's where we were introduced to our drill instructor. The minute I saw him, I knew we were in trouble. He was one of the hardest looking men I've ever met, lean and trim and tough as ten-penny nails. He had the appearance of case hardened steel. But the look in his eyes sent chills down my spine. They were emotionless, the sinister slits of a killer, the cold, calculating look of a reef shark. By the way he stared straight through us, we could see that he didn't give a flip whether we lived or died.

I remember him dispassionately scanning the ranks of sweating volunteers. I thought I detected the slightest hint of a smile as he took inventory of his latest crop of victims. Gone were the verbal abuse and crude obscenities of boot camp; the protocol had a more polished and professional air. Our physical fitness instructor announced, "You people have been given the privilege of demonstrating the highest examples of patriotic sacrifice. We are offering you the maximum opportunity to give your life for your country. Those of you who prove you have what it takes will be accepted. The rest of you will not. From this day forward, you will be required to give whatever we require. Naval Special Forces is an elite team whose members have shown the pride and determination to be a part. If you think you have what it takes to cut it, I want you to understand that the days of the regular navy are now over. Is that understood?" We all responded with a resounding, "Yes sir!," which of course was not enthusiastic enough and had to be repeated several times until the proper decibel level was reached.

For our opening ordeal, we were lined up five abreast and ten deep, and ordered into a doubletime jog echoing crude "Jody" calls as our tormentor ran circles around us calling cadences and taunting the weak. The first minute of novelty and esprit-de-corps soon evaporated in the searing heat as he quickened the pace and drove us down an endless stretch of loose sandy beach. The pain began to take its toll. While grinding us into the sand he jogged on almost effortlessly. Glistening beads of sweat poured from our faces, sending briny rivulets stinging into our eyes. Crotches, armpits, and the small of our backs were drenched in sweat as we gulped air like grounded carp. I felt like my chest was going to explode. I was literally on the verge of collapse. Our orderly ranks had disintegrated into a convulsive mass of panting men. It was back to Bataan all over. When I thought I could take no more, our tormentor ordered an abrupt halt. Men slumped to the ground in utter exhaustion or bent with hands on their knees, gasping for air. I remember that same, almost imperceptible trace of a smirk on the instructor's lips as he mockingly inquired, "Well men, are you having fun yet?" The whole experience was like a controlled heart attack. I remember thinking, "I must have been out of my mind to have gotten myself into this nut house."

Our death run was only the first of countless exercises maniacally structured to weed out the weak. Over the ensuing weeks we hit the exercise field at 6 A.M. every morning where we were subjected to endless rounds of muscle burning, gut cramping, chest ripping calisthenics designed to make us or break us. It seemed that a Darwinian philosophy prevailed, stressing the survival of the fittest. Short of murder, everything was done to eliminate those who couldn't survive. We were constantly reminded that we had received a round trip ticket to Coronado and could leave any time we pleased. All you had to do was ring the infamous ship's bell outside the instructor's shack. Some exercised their option with no regrets, some had nervous breakdowns from the mental pressure and ended up in a psych ward. Others were dropped because of broken bones. Still others never made it back to the mainland alive.

There were life threatening hazards involved for those who would undergo underwater phases of training. No one was attacked in the shark infested waters, but some were lost in the swift currents or treacherous undertows during two mile swims to shore in nighttime seaborne assaults. Others drowned when they panicked in U.D.T. training.

At the end of the physical training phase, I learned that I was heading to the Naval Special Operations Group— S.O.G. for short, which operated in Southeast Asia. Some of those who survived the conditioning phase would be assigned to Basic Underwater Demolitions School, while others would proceed to SEAL training. Others went to jump school at Fort Benning, while still others went to Marine Sniper School at Camp Pendleton. For a guy who didn't want to go to college, I sure was spending a lot of time in schools! I was selected to be a part of Naval Special Forces assigned to Riverene Special Warfare Group. The Naval Special Warfare Group was in the process of forming a special operations group similar to S.O.G. counterparts in the Army Special Forces. Though we were not officially designated as SEALS we trained alongside them and worked with SEALS commando teams as a part of our covert activities in 'Nam.

In 'Nam, Naval S.O.G. units operated under the Special Forces umbrella of the Military Assistance Command Vietnam/Studies and Observations Group (MACV/SOG). This was a cover designation to conceal its real purpose and identity. The term "Special Operations Group" more accurately reflected the clandestine nature of S.O.G.

S.O.G. teams were highly classified counterinsurgency units fighting a covert war, often deep within enemy territory. It was a top-secret side to Vietnam you didn't read about in the papers back home. Their orders often bypassed the normal channels of military command and came directly from CIA headquarters in Langley, Virginia, as well as the highest echelons of the U.S. government including the Oval Office. The main headquarters of S.O.G. was located at Tan Son Nhut Airbase on the outskirts of Saigon. While missions were usually planned there, they were generally implemented and launched by small, highly trained units from Forward Operation Bases (F.O.B.'s) scattered throughout the provinces of Vietnam. Missions ran the gauntlet of covert activities from assassinations and kidnapping of enemy personnel, sabotage and ambushes, the retrieval of sensitive documents or top secret equipment, and covert cross-border incursions into Burma, Cambodia, Laos, North Vietnam, and the Provinces of Yunman, Kwangsi, Kwangtung, and Hainan Island in China to carry out intelligence gathering or raids on strategic installations in enemy territory.

7

Mare Island

After a grueling month at Coronado, my unit was transferred to Naval Inshore Operations Training Center at Mare Island Naval Base located north of San Francisco Bay. The sights and sounds of the Bay area were a dramatic contrast to Coronado. The forlorn baritone of Fort Baker's fog horn, the mist shrouded towers of the Golden Gate, the steelwool columns of fog which crawled over the coastal mountains, the panoramic night skyline which sparkled like a million starlit crystals, and the salt laden breezes white capping across San Pablo Bay would also be a welcome respite before the harsh extremes of survival training.

The change was refreshing, as much by the times as the ambience of the City by the Bay. You could almost feel a contagious electricity in the air. The bay was the cradle of Berkeley and Haight and the "Flower Children." The city was still basking in the euphoria of the "Summer of Love." Everything seemed to be drawn by a mystical force. "Are You Going to San Francisco?" seemed to beckon with a captivating allurement. It was calling you more to a state of mind than a physical location—a place to drop out and tune in to a surrealistic world of naive illusions. But I was too gung ho and far removed from the dreamy headspace to relate. I was passing through in my inevitable passage to 'Nam and another world of warped realities.

At Mare Island we undertook Riverene Warfare Training in swift, maneuverable, shallow draft PBR boats (patrol boats river) which were being used extensively in the "brown water navy" to navigate the inland waterways and canals of Vietnam. The 31' fiberglass boats were compact but heavily armed with a twin .50 caliber gun turret in the bow, a single .50 caliber machine gun aft, and an M-60 machine gun and a 40mm grenade launcher mounted amidships. Besides the heavy weapons, each boat carried a well-stocked arsenal of M-16's, shotguns, claymores, and grenades of every description—plenty of lethal toys for bored teenagers to play with when the monotonous interludes of war got the best of them. In 'Nam, we even resorted to waterskiing when the routine got too dull.

Each boat had a complement of four men—an engine man, a coxswain to run the boat, a gunner's mate to maintain the guns, and a boatswain's mate for general maintenance. I was a bit of an oddity because I had been cross qualified as both a Marine corpsman and a Navy Commando.

For a couple of months we operated out of Mare Island navigating the marshy inlets of San Pablo Bay and the tree-lined sloughs of the San Joaquin Delta. We staged simulated patrols, SEAL team extractions, and participated in night ambushes in the backwater canals and jungle-like islands of the delta. We also learned how to operate the radio; requesting artillery strikes, dust-offs, and relaying information.

When we weren't plying the choppy waters of San Pablo Bay or the Carquinez Straights, we were taking a battery of classroom and in-the-field courses to prepare us for

Vietnam. Some courses taught us about communist ideology, the Viet Cong infrastructure, and V.C. tactics. We were given a historical and political overview of Vietnam and the reasons for our involvement. In the early '60s, Special Forces advisors had been dispatched to offer assistance to the South Vietnamese government in their war against the Viet Cong. But the war had escalated to a point where it seemed the only thing keeping the government from toppling was enormous infusions of U.S. dollars and adolescent blood. The massive American buildup to half a million men was in response to the growing flood of men and materials flowing southward along the Ho Chi Minh Trail from communist stockpiles in the north. The war had grown dirty for both sides, leading to the covert involvement of U.S. forces to thwart the growing menace from the north. If they were going to play dirty, then we would play by their rules.

We were also qualified on a variety of weapons ranging from machine guns and automatic weapons to pistols, grenades, M-79 grenade launchers, flame throwers, L.A.W. rockets, and an assortment of specialized paraphernalia like the Starlight Scope. A special emphasis was placed on the firing, breakdown, cleaning, and assembly of the M-l6. We were also familiarized with the Russian AK-47 assault rifle, and an array of Chi-Com and communist bloc weapons we might encounter and utilize in 'Nam.

We were shown examples of simple, but diabolically effective booby traps resourcefully constructed by the Viet Cong out of anything from bamboo to discarded C-ration cans. We learned how to make our own homemade booby traps, where to place them and how to conceal them. We were shown how to cut needle sharp punji sticks, how to harden them over a fire and dip them in excrement to produce gangrene in the wound. For demolition, we also learned how to rig C-4 and claymores.

Another facet of our training involved a healthy dose of in-the-field exposure to tactics and strategy. We learned how to set up night defensive positions, where to place machine guns and establish fields of fire. We practiced setting up ambushes like the classic horseshoe and "L" shaped ambush. We even had mock firefights with our SEAL instructors dressing up like V.C. and ambushing us while we were on patrol or attacking us at night while we were beached in the delta.

We were also given basic hand-to-hand demonstrations. We were shown how to use a rope or piano wire to garrote an opponent. A host of brutal, but effective, methods to eliminate the enemy quickly and efficiently were demonstrated.

We also received hands on training in the science of killing someone with our K-bar knives. Our instructors would demonstrate the proper procedure in stop frame steps. The attacker's hand would be placed over the victim's mouth from behind. The head would be pulled up and back, thus exposing the neck. Then, with a quick diagonal slice from top to bottom, the carotid artery, which carries blood directly to the brain, is severed. It was messy, but blackout and death follow within seconds.

In the second method, the victim is also attacked from the rear. This time, however, the attacker reaches around from behind, cups his hand under the chin and jerks the head backward. At the same time, he drives his knife between the 4th and 5th vertebrae, severing the spinal cord and causing instant paralysis and death.

We were also introduced to newly devised "quick-kill" methods birthed by the unique combat conditions found in the jungles of 'Nam. You were fighting at such close quarters that you had to react with lightning speed and accuracy to survive. We learned how to carry our M-16's and shotguns at waist level with such a natural heft that they seemed like an extension of our bodies. We learned to swing and shoot from the hip at a moment's notice. We were actually taken to a firing range and given Daisy BB guns to fine tune our reflexes. An instructor would stand about ten feet in front of us and to the side. On command, he would toss a coin into the air. We would shoot from the hip without sight aiming. The angle, speed and trajectory were all calculated in a split second by the brain. What is amazing is the fact that we learned to hit the coin eight out of ten times. A couple of men actually maxed the exercise.

And throughout our training we were instilled with the militant passion to be aggressive—to take the battle to the enemy, to never yield. When fired upon, we were told never to "hit the dirt." Instead, incoming fire was to serve as a signal for us to fire back and assault. Our overriding strategy was, "the best defense is a good offense." Never give ground.

But, probably the most beneficial by-product of our Riverene training was the sense of teamwork which began to develop as we cooperated in the task of manning our boats. Each man was a professional who soon learned the importance of teamwork. We not only learned how to do our own primary tasks proficiently, but learned other unique responsibilities as well, in case one of our crewmates got hit in a fire fight. Because of the constant risk of death, we were all forced to be versatile. After a few weeks, we all grew so adept at our duties that they became second nature. But not only did we develop a synchronized proficiency in our shipboard skills, we also developed a deep sense of camaraderie. It was an intimate marriage of skills and esprit.

As our training reached the halfway point, the anticipation of going to 'Nam mounted. After 15 weeks of training, we no longer wanted to forestall the inevitable. We just wanted to get our training over and get on with it. It seemed like we spent a lot of nights at the EM Club on base; drinking beer, listening to "Cream" and "The Doors," and finding a safe harbor in one another's conversation as we waited for the clock to run out.

On weekend liberties, we sought other diversions to occupy our time. Sometimes we would catch the bus to Berkeley to check out the anti-war protestors thronging Telegraph Avenue. But we found more carefree activities in the city hanging out of the cable cars and savoring the sights and smells of Chinatown and Fisherman's Wharf.

We got a special, if not perverted, curiosity out of checking out the hippies. We'd stroll the sidewalks of Haight Ashbury with the same incredulous expressions of sightseers who would cruise the Haight in tour buses gawking at the street people like they were aliens from another planet. The sidewalks were thronged with wall-to-wall freaks dressed in all manner of weird apparel. Their slapdash attire looked like a mob had ransacked a thrift store, adding the finishing touches to their outlandish garb by cleaning out a costume shop. Dressed in my straight civies with my regulation haircut, I didn't know who looked more out of place.

On some weekends, I just wanted to get away from the circus atmosphere of the bay and the petty harassment of base duty. I'd take the bus to San Jose and simply crash out and vegetate at my aunt and uncle's.

The weeks of close quarter training had bonded the crews like epoxy. We had worked hard, pulled together and learned to depend on one another. We were tight and ready. Most of us were equals. We were peers on the same wavelength. But we didn't share that trust and camaraderie with our officers. Whether the navy intended to or not, our training began to establish a pattern in our relationships with officers. We were a tight knit group of enlisted men without the rank or privileges of our superiors. I suppose the gulf which existed between enlisted men and officers has always existed and seldom been bridged.

The fact that they segregated themselves from us, often with a conceited air of indifference, did little to alleviate the growing sense of suspicion and resentment we felt toward them and the system. Officers seldom fraternized with the lower ranks of enlisted men. They were the nobility, we were the commoners. They had their clubs and mess halls and insignia, and we had ours. We recognized the need for chains of command, obedience and respect for authority, but the navy's version of the caste system had a subtle way of backfiring. It was offensive enough submitting to the petty rules and regulations of stateside duty, but things got especially galling when we were forced to bear the unconventional burdens of Vietnam rear area pogues and "by the book" officers who had no consciousness of the sacrifices we were making.

The alienation and contempt was not just due to petty rules or rank. There was an inherent distrust toward most of our officers. In all the armies of the world, it's the common grunt who does the dirty work. They may have had their college degrees and officer's training, but most of the responsibility fell upon our shoulders. It's the lowly dog-face and grunt who spills the blood and guts, while ambitious career officers and desk jockey lifers get the glory. We had our officers who put their men first before promotions and medals, but we had more than our share of self-serving glory boys whose greatest physical sacrifices involved sweating behind a typewriter banging out mythical reports of their gallantry and heroism under fire. While they busied themselves with the rigors of paper pushing and garnishing medals, we were slopping through the killing zone, laying our lives on the line. Most of our officers were so green or inept that we dreaded taking them on patrol with us, lest they screw up and get us wasted. By the time we were fully immersed in the paddy lands of 'Nam we'd lost respect for officers in general. We were just fed up with being jerked around by the system.

8

Survival, Evasion, Resistance, Escape

After three months of preparatory training at Mare Island, my unit was transferred to S.E.R.E. school—"Survival, Evasion, Resistance, and Escape." It represented the final "on the job" training phase where we would put into practice much of the instruction we had received at Mare Island. S.E.R.E. school was divided into three phases designed to equip us with survival skills we might require in three principal climate zones. The first stage involved woodland survival in the rain forests of Whidbey Island in Washington state, no doubt to prepare us for possible conditions we might encounter in Europe or Russia. The second phase was held in the arid deserts of Baja California. The third phase was jungle survival at Cubic Point in the Philippines.

In each location, we were taught the fine arts of survival. We learned to adapt to the environment, to depend upon our ingenuity and resourcefulness. We were taught how to camouflage ourselves, move by stealth, and become one with the land. We learned simple techniques for snaring indigenous game with handmade traps and piano wire. We were forced to live off the land. We ate snakes, lizards, monkeys, mussels, roots, rabbits, and just about anything a wild goat would find edible. In the desert, we learned how to conserve water and where to find it. We learned to maneuver through jungle so dense you couldn't see more than a few feet in front of you. We learned to use compasses and shoot azimuths and find our way back after we had been dropped off miles from nowhere in desolate and inhospitable terrain.

It was all very serious, but still a far cry from the lethal conditions of 'Nam. In training, we may have run out of water or food or lost our way in the woods or gotten captured in mock war games or screwed up somehow, but we were still being shepherded and chaperoned by the protective oversight of our instructors.

However, S.E.R.E. school was a reasonable foretaste of conditions S.O.G. teams would be required to acclimate themselves to in 'Nam if they wanted to beat Charlie at his own game. In 'Nam some teams adjusted themselves to the same Spartan existence as the Viet Cong. On some missions they traded in the standard garb of the typical combat grunt—nylon and leather jungle boots, baggy, deep-pocketed jungle fatigues, nylon rucksack, M-16, flak jacket, steel helmet with camouflage cover, and C-rations—in favor of black pajamas, AK assault rifles, conical hats and gluttonous balls of rice.

But above and beyond basic survival techniques, one of the primary aspects of our training involved the art of escape, resistance, and evasion. Our instructors had built a simulated North Vietnamese prison camp. Ex-P.O.W.'s from Korea and vets who had done one or two tours in 'Nam served as our guards and interrogators. Many of them were Japanese and Chinese Americans who were used to impersonate North Vietnamese guards. Their experience added an extra touch of authenticity. They dressed in the distinctive dull green uniforms of the North Vietnamese with pith helmets and brass buckles emblazoned

with a red star. The camps were depressing affairs surrounded by barbed wire, wooden guard towers, and bel-
ligerent guards toting AK-47's. It conjured up black and
white images of Japanese internment camps from some
old war movie.

Our captors handed each of us a K-bar, a strand of piano
wire, and a compass. We were given a head start. Our
task was to escape and evade capture by living off the land.
It was easy getting into the game. I remember the thrill of
the chase as I scrambled into the surrounding jungle; pur-
sued by our guards, stalked by an unseen predator, playing
the cat and mouse game of hide and seek.

In all of our attempts at evasion, the jungle was the most
challenging environment, maybe because it came the closest to conditions we would soon encounter in Vietnam.

But the jungle was a foreboding refuge; dark and sinister. Except for an occasional splinter of sunlight which
penetrated the triple canopy, I soon found myself smothered in a dappled maze of green twilight. The jungle gave
the impression of being swallowed up in a shadowy un-
derworld of living matter. It was an ominous place of eternal shadows. In places, the lush foliage was almost
impenetrable—so densely compacted it was nearly claustrophobic. It was a congested maze of bamboo stalks clumped
together like bundles of lime green pillars and enormous
broad leaves the size of elephant ears. At every turn, it
manifested a hostile, almost alien-like character.

It was a deceptive place of incredible beauty and unyielding danger. Tree trunks and stems were ensnarled
with twisting vines which seemed to be strangling the life
out of their competitors. Creepers dangled like limp ten-
acles from branches, while overhead, gnarled vines snaked
off through the clotted vegetation. The trees and foliage
were damp and dripping from the perpetual humidity. Everything appeared to be sweating in nervous anticipation.
It was a place of death. The pungent decomposing smell
of rotting vegetation seemed to accent the atmosphere.

Except for the occasional sounds of men, the only noises came from the irritating whine of hungry insects or the exotic sounds of trilling birds high in the overhead canopy.

The game grew more serious with each passing hour. I sought to elude my pursuers by staying off of the occasional footpath or animal track I encountered, ever watchful for vipers and poisonous spiders. I remember creeping catlike through the clotted tangle pricked by the unnerving sensation of unseen specters closing in. Every nerve ending, every muscle, every sinew was tensed in anticipation of fight or flight. My system was electrified with ample doses of adrenaline which seemed to heighten primal instincts. I was on that cutting edge of suspense where your mind functions smoother, your thoughts are more lucid, your reflexes more adroit. I can remember moving almost imperceptibly through the thick foliage. Every few paces, I'd pause to look and listen—eyes darting purposely back and forth, scrutinizing every color, every contour for an irregularity in the jungle's symmetry before continuing. My brain sifted every shred of stimuli for potential danger—the rustling of palm fronds, the faint snap of a twig, the gentle sound of a footfall.

It was an elaborate game of hide and seek which taxed your resourcefulness. Some of the guys really got into it. At times it seemed so authentic that you wondered whether our pursuers were psychotically replaying roles from their past.

Our trackers hunted us down with the dogged determination of Gestapo agents, even shooting over our heads to heighten the sense of reality. If we evaded capture within the allotted time, we turned ourselves in to the camp commandant. After our surrender or capture, we were subjected to what was referred to as the "problem." The "problem" was a P.O.W. period of physical and psychological harassment designed to wear us down and cause us to break.

Our arms were trussed behind our backs at the elbows.

Then our guards would begin their interrogation by hanging us upside down in a 55-gallon drum of water with blocks of ice floating on top. Most of us would thrash in defiance as they held us under until the last bubbles broke the surface, then they would pull us out gasping for air and coughing up water. They had the timing down to a science. They'd take us right to the brink of panic. They were pushing us to our limits of psychological endurance in methodic stages. As soon as we were pulled from our mock drowning, our interrogators were in our faces screaming insults and questions interlaced with communist propaganda—all to demoralize and break our spirit.

After the ice water dunkings, we were taken to the "hot box." They were tiny enclosures measuring 2-½′ × 4-½′. They were made out of corrugated metal and had the appearance of the hot box used in the movie "Bridge on the River Kwai," except ours were smaller. We were forced head first on our hands and knees into the box, then the lid would be locked. Except for a couple dusty pin shafts of light from nail holes, it was pitch black inside. The sun beating down on the metal siding drove the temperature to oppressive extremes. It was like crawling head first into an oven and having the door shut. I felt like a turkey basting in my own sweat. They'd leave you in the box broiling in the stifling heat for several hours. It took extreme mental discipline to fight back the tide of claustrophobic panic which threatened to engulf us with each passing moment.

When your head wasn't being held under the water, your body stuffed into the hot box, or you weren't standing at attention in an open pen for hours in the rain, we were dragged into cramped interrogation rooms with bright red lights where we were slapped around and verbally assaulted and threatened for hours on end. To weaken our resistance, we were deprived of sleep and given no food for several days. After a while the acting took on a frightening air of reality.

The brainwashing and harassment was relentless. If they weren't blaring mournful Vietnamese music or propaganda speeches through the camp loud speakers, they were constantly lining us up for inspection. We were filthy from exercising in the dirt and mud and smelling pretty ripe from the hot box, so we never passed. It didn't take much to give our guards an excuse to punch our lights out. A blow to the stomach or a few slaps across the face was sufficient humiliation. After what seemed a couple of weeks, we were half-starved, half-zombie-like men who had taken on the look of actual P.O.W.'s, wearied and haggard in their appearance. It had gotten to the point that it was hard discerning where reality ended and make-believe began. The mental and physical strain reached a point where you lost track of time and space. Your singleminded goal boiled down to making it through one day at a time.

Everything humanly possible, within the fragile limits of the law, was done to break us. Some snapped like a brittle pencil when forced to bend too far. They may have endured the physical pressures of Coronado, but the mental and emotional ordeal of P.O.W. captivity was too much to bear. They simply cracked under the strain.

The knowledge that they could quit the ordeal at any point became an irresistible temptation to some. It's easy to fantasize about your fortitude. Everyone likes to think they can bear a little more pain, starve a little longer, show a bit more courage than the next guy. But private illusions of physical and mental prowess seldom measure up to expectations when put to the test.

This was my greatest fear—the fear of psychologically losing it. No one ever mentioned it, but we all knew that it was the common denominator lurking beneath the surface of our conversations. In spite of all of our boast and bravado, none of us knew the limits of our endurance. It wasn't so much the fear of dying in combat or getting wounded or even facing capture that troubled me. It was that inner tug-of-war between cowardice and courage which resides deep in the recesses of every man. It's every man's version of Stephen Crane's *Red Badge of Courage*. It's the nagging uncertainty which may never be known: "Will I break under torture?"; "Will I prove a coward?"; "Will my finger hesitate on the trigger?" It was troubling questions such as these which tormented men during private moments of reflection. When all was said and done, we feared cowardice more than the unknown.

I think only two things kept me going; the fear of failure and the coveted Black Beret of the Naval Special Forces. They served as the carrot and the whip.

At unpredictable moments someone would abruptly crack. They would collapse or freak out or simply start screaming. The hot box got a lot of them. There's something terrifying about claustrophobia. The suffocating fear of claustrophobic confinement begins to gnaw on hidden phobias, wearing away at frayed nerves and tired minds until it builds like the growing swell of an oncoming breaker. Then it overwhelms you in an uncontrollable wave of panic.

Everyone had a number. When you went into the box, a guard would periodically check the boxes. If you were "losing it" you were instructed to bang on the box. If you were asked to give your number and didn't respond, they would pull you out. In that event, you were washed out. Some fainted from heat stroke. Several suffered heart seizures.

I remember one guy who flipped out during an interrogation session. He spilled his guts to the interrogators. When they brought him back to our barracks, we got all over him for betraying information. At that point he came apart at the seams. He fell on his knees and started screaming like he was insane. He had a nervous breakdown. The guards rushed into the barracks, put his clothes on him, and took him away, no doubt, to some nut ward. He was a complete basket case.

They were extremely prompt in disposing of the guy. I

suspected they were a little freaked themselves that the hysteria might be contagious. They knew they were pushing the realism to the limits. Things were very volatile and could backfire at any moment. Nobody can play with fire forever without getting burned. Our captors had a healthy respect for the possibilities that their prisoners would only take so much abuse before cracking or retaliating against their tormentors. The possibility of turning the tables on our guards became more tempting with every passing day. It wouldn't be the first time they carried the game too far.

In fact, we were briefed by the Air Force before we were sent to the P.O.W. camp, because we were a new batch of Riverene Commandos. The Air Force actually ran the camp. They made us promise not to take it over. They'd learned the hard way that some prisoners could be like wild tigers in captivity—just waiting for the opportunity to turn on their handlers. They were playing a game which could get ugly real quick. A SEAL team before us were a bunch of animals. Not only did most of them escape, but they regrouped and came back to capture the prison. They made the camp commander and guards eat the same medicine they had dished out themselves. They beat them up and threw them into the "box" in reprisal. What is more, they got so caught up in the charade that they refused to let them go. The Navy had to fly in a high ranking officer and literally beg the SEAL team commander to set his prisoners free. The whole episode was a major embarrassment to the military. It got so real, it got out of hand.

Through fear of failure and sheer endurance, I managed to gut out the "problem." Each morning we had been herded into the compound and ordered to stand at attention before the camp commandant, who was peacocking on the platform. We were forced to stand before the North Vietnamese flag while the mournful oriental sounds of their national anthem screeched over the loud speaker. Even then, we would stand in subdued defiance spitting or farting or screwing our faces in parodies of contempt. It was subtle enough not to get our faces smashed in by a bully guard, but it was still a small token of our resistance.

None of us knew when the last day of the "problem" would arrive. They purposely left it indefinite to play on the sense of hopelessness and uncertainty. But one morning we were mustered into formation like all the previous mornings almost oblivious to ritual. Few of us took note at first that the camp commandant was no longer dressed in a North Vietnamese uniform. Gone too was the pompous look of lordship. Instead, he was standing erect with a proud patriotic look, wearing the American uniform of a full bird colonel.

Most of our senses had been so dulled by the ordeal that few noticed that the stars and stripes were flapping on the pole where the North Vietnamese flag had flown. Exhaustion and a lack of food for over a week had left us in a dazed stupor. At first, his words failed to register, "Gentlemen, the problem is over." That's when "The Star Spangled-Banner" began to play through the camp speaker. It was a moment of emotional catharsis. A wave of patriotism suddenly swept over the ragged ranks. Men who had endured physical and mental abuse in stoic defiance, suddenly broke. Warm tears of gratitude and relief coursed down grimy, smiling faces. The whole ordeal was a profound revelation of the price of liberty. In a minute way, we had each tasted of the sacrifices others had made to make our nation free.

9

Welcome To Vietnam!

My simmering contempt for nit-picky officers reached a flash point on the eve of my departure. When we completed S.E.R.E. training in the Philippines, we were sent to Vietnamese Language School at Coronado for a one month crash course while our final orders were being processed. When our orders were cut, we learned that we would be shipping out the following Tuesday. It meant I only had one more weekend to party in the land of the "Big PX" until they sent us to the armpit.

But some lame brain officer assigned me to weekend duty confined to Coronado. "Great," I thought to myself. "I'm probably going to get blown away and never come back, and some officer wants me to stand weekend duty guarding this stupid base." Well, I wasn't about to spend my last few hours in the world sitting on my rear. Weekend liberty usually ran from 4:00 P.M. Friday afternoon to check-in time Sunday evening. I decided that since some clerk officer expected me to pull weekend duty, I might as well make a long weekend out of it, so I went A.W.O.L. Thursday night and headed for my aunt's house in San

Jose. As far as I was concerned, I had nothing to lose. After all, what were they going to do to me, send me to Vietnam? Besides, if by some stroke of providence the system malfunctioned and they ended up keeping me in the states, they would be doing me a big favor.

I spent the weekend partying down with my uncle. He'd been in the navy and was determined to give this sailor one last fling. I was no longer their little nephew Mickey, but a young man who had earned their respect.

I pulled to a stop at the entrance gate to Coronado Monday morning a bit hung over and green at the gills. When I handed my I.D. card to one of the Marine Corps M.P.'s, he checked some names on a clipboard and said, "Ah, ha, we've been looking for you, Block." It was a tense moment. I didn't know if they were going to use their nightsticks to work me over. The interservice rivalry between the Marine Corps and the Navy reaches back to the days of Tripoli and the Halls of Montezuma. They probably assumed they had another swabby on their hands who needed to be taught a lesson. They were acting real tough, jumping in my face and reading me the riot act. But I wasn't some dumb deckhand, and I still had nothing to lose. As soon as the M.P. caught his breath, I climbed back in his face and shouted, "Hey, you dogbreath jarhead, I'm leaving for Vietnam tomorrow. You're crazy if you think I'm going to hang around here and guard this base!"

As soon as they heard that, they changed their tune. They put me in a jeep and drove me over to my barracks and said goodbye. When my C.O. heard I was back, he came over to tell me that I had been written up, but added with a wink, "You're in luck, Block, we're all leaving together tomorrow at three o'clock from Travis Air Force Base." At least our C.O. had a streak of humanity.

At ten o'clock the following morning, I was brought before Captain's Mast in front of the Base Commander to hear my charges of A.W.O.L. read. But as far as I was concerned, the verdict was a foregone conclusion. When the Old Man finished reading the charges, he laid the papers on his desk and said, "Do you have anything to say for yourself?" "Sir, I'm leaving for Vietnam this afternoon at three o'clock. Chances are I won't be coming back. Would you sit in this base on your last weekend if you knew you probably weren't coming back, or would you take your best shot?"

He looked at me with a gleam in his eye. "Good point." "Sir, if you don't want me to go to Vietnam, it's fine with me, but I doubt whether there's time to change my orders. Besides, the Navy hasn't paid for all this training so I can rot in the brig." He paused for a moment then responded with an obvious tone of sarcasm (you could almost commit murder with immunity in our outfit), "Well, in view of your exemplary record, you've never been in too much trouble before, I will suspend your sentence until your next duty station. Your next commanding officer can reopen your case and pass sentence." That was the pre-arranged loophole. Since my next C.O. would be my present C.O., all I'd have to do is buy the Old Man a bottle of Jack Daniel's and my A.W.O.L. charges would be history.

I spent the rest of the morning packing my gear and getting ready to pull out. At about three, a couple of navy blue buses pulled up outside our barracks and we lugged our gear aboard. We were a pretty wild looking bunch. Guys carried duffle bags containing shoulder holsters and concealed combat knives. Some had .357 magnums and one guy even had a pump shotgun he'd purchased from a sporting goods store. Whiskey bottles and six-packs were hanging out of our duffle bags. We looked like a cross between the Road Warriors and the Dirty Dozen. But we had a "who cares" attitude. Like I said, "what were they going to do, send us to Vietnam?"

The PSA stewardesses were pretty freaked out when they saw us climbing up the rear boarding ramp. But there wasn't much they could do, we were armed and dangerous with military clearance.

When we got to Travis, our orders and shot cards were double checked to make sure they were up to date. By the time they shipped you to 'Nam, you had endured eighteen to twenty injections including yellow fever, typhoid, tetanus, and plague shots. We guarded our shot cards with our lives. If you lost it, they made you take them all over again.

After the final processing check, we were herded into a sectioned off area in the terminal to await our plane. We were a mixed lot of marines and air force personnel. Most of the men were clustered in small groups, smoking and fidgeting. A few were shucking and jiving while they took turns playing amateur comedian. Most of them were spit and polish types in pressed uniforms with the solitary red and yellow National Defense ribbon pinned on their chests. They were "Remington Raiders" heading for kickback jobs in safe rear areas. They stood out in stark contrast to my outfit who stood off to one side drinking beer and scotch from our private commissary, getting high for the big party on the way over. We were making sure we would be feeling no pain by the time we arrived in 'Nam.

About an hour before our plane landed, families started arriving to greet the husbands and sons and brothers who were returning from their tour. The atmosphere suddenly turned sedated. Except for a few awkward spurts of laughter, most of the conversation took on a subdued, almost solemn, quietness. We all knew the hour was at hand. The atmosphere was taut and tense as men tried to act calm and together with a James Dean indifference. But, most were poor performers who only managed to highlight their nervousness rather than conceal it.

More than an hour passed before the DC-8 touched down and taxied to a stop in front of the terminal. I took one look at the big bird and knew I was about to step through the looking glass. The commercial charter jet was one of those new "Braniff" jets painted with psychedelic colors. I remember thinking that Vietnam had to be a pretty unusual place to be sending us there in a psychedelic jet.

In a few moments, a line of returning soldiers began to stream down the boarding ramp and into the lobby. A respectful silence settled over our group. It was like the senior varsity was passing in solemn review before the freshman class. They shuffled into the terminal in rumpled khakis, sporting an assortment of berets and jump boots, C.I.B.'s and the conspicuous row of green and white and yellow and red campaign ribbons. A few had an additional row of Purple Hearts, Bronze Stars and Air Medals. They wore unit patches of yellow and black, blue and red, red and green.

They all arrived in a state of tired euphoria. Some had only been out of the field for 36 hours. Each of their eyes were circled with dark hollows. They were the same age as we, but looked much older.

Some seemed oblivious to our presence, others cast us a weary, sad-eyed glance. A few gave us a grim smile. A handful of Marines in our group were asking, "Hey man, what is it like over there?" or "How many gooks did you waste?" Most responded with blank expressions. A few shook their heads and taunted them with gallows humor, "You cherries are going to be sorrryyy," "Only 365 days to go," or "When you get your legs blown off can I have your boots?"

We waited a few more minutes while our jet was being refueled. When the order was given to board, we marched across the tarmac to the waiting plane. It was eerie. Except for the cadence of boots hitting the asphalt in unison, no one said a word. The moment we had been waiting for for months had arrived.

I remember the silhouette of the bird waiting like an apparition on the runway, the rolling oak studded hills already turning saffron in the late spring sun, and the cool gusts of sea breeze from the Carquinez Straights kicking through the ranks. It was the longest walk of our lives. We all knew that some were taking their last steps on American soil.

In a few minutes we would take off and another transport would land, bearing a cargo load of processed bodies from the morgue units in 'Nam on their way to military funerals in Sacramento, Missoula, Birmingham, Chicago, El Paso, and a thousand grieving crossroads scattered throughout our country.

The stewardesses were polite but reserved, not because we were red-blooded males who would not see another round-eyed woman in a year, but because they had already shuttled too many young men over and back. They had seen too many bewildered faces. Because they knew that some would not return alive, they couldn't look us in the eyes. It was like someone had passed gas in a crowd, and everyone was too embarrassed to say anything. So we avoided the obvious, stuffed our gear in the storage compartments, and prepared for the trip over.

In moments, we raced down the runway and climbed into the Pacific sky headed for our first stopover in Hawaii. As soon as the ''No Smoking'' and ''Fasten Your Seat Belts'' signs were off, we broke out the booze and started to party down. The crew offered no protests. They'd been on too many such flights to quibble about company rules.

When we landed in Honolulu, we spent a couple of hours stretching our legs in a roped off area waiting for our plane to be serviced and refueled. Ten hours later, worn out by cramped seats and intoxicated jet-lag, we began our descent into Clark Air Force Base in the Philippines for a final refueling. It was a brain baking 110 degrees when we stepped off the plane—so hot that the lush green mountains surrounding the base shimmered in the morning heat.

It was a strange sensation, surveying the same mountains my father had fought his way over 24 years before in

MacArthur's race to liberate Manila. Only the South China Sea separated me from my war. I couldn't help wondering how ours would differ. Oddly enough, I still entertained notions of coming back a hero and making my dad proud; as if in some subtle way my going would bring our lives full circle to a new start.

Our stopover was short lived. In moments, we were reboarded, strapped in, and airborne over blue water. There had been an almost festive spirit on board until we lifted off the runway at Clark Field. But, as we climbed to 30,000 feet over the South China Sea, the mood suddenly sobered. The jocular mood of jubilant soldiers who had been boasting of their killer instincts and combat bravado suddenly vanished. Men were now silent, lost in the private inventory of their manhood. Some stared glumly out their windows. Others stared at the seat in front of them. All were wondering, "Will I make the return flight a year from now? Will I come home early without arms or legs or eyes? Will I be shipped home in a box?" We all considered the questions for which there were no answers.

A little over an hour passed when the green coastline of Vietnam slipped beneath us. The stewardess's announcement arrested our attention, "Gentlemen, please extinguish cigarettes and fasten your seat belts. We are beginning our final descent into Saigon. On behalf of Braniff Airlines, we want to welcome you to the Republic of Vietnam."

Through a broken cover of cotton-like clouds, we could see Saigon stretching in a cluttered patchwork for miles. A blanket of haze and smoke gave it a dirty appearance. I felt the pitch of the engines change as the pilot gained altitude and banked to the left. As the fuselage tilted, I noticed the sun's reflection glinting off the metal roots and river snaking through the city. We continued to bank in wide gentle circles for several minutes before the pilot came on the intercom and said, "Gentlemen, this is the pilot, ah, we are circling at 8,000 feet over Saigon until we receive a clearance to land. The V.C. are mortaring Tan Son Nhut Airbase.'' We all looked at each other with that "you got to be kidding me" look.

After a half hour of circling, we began our approach. No sooner had the wheels of our jet screeched on the runway when the pilot announced, "Gentlemen, when we stop, we want you to promptly exit the plane. The shelling could resume at any minute."

When we stepped from the plane, the heat hit us like a blast furnace. Stepping from the air conditioned crispness of cabin air into the sweltering heat and humidity of 'Nam was like stepping into a steam room. I was instantly slick with sweat. Our foreheads glistened with beads of perspiration, sending rivulets of brine pouring down our faces and necks, soaking our uniforms and stinging our eyes. It was my introduction to the fact that you were always sweating in Vietnam—everything sweated in 'Nam. Not only was the heat unbearable, but the air was fouled with the acrid stench of smoke, burnt gunpowder, rusting metal, petroleum products, and excrement. My first impressions of the country were offensive.

Under the barks of watchful sergeants, we were herded toward a briefing building surrounded by sandbags and 55 gallon drums. As we walked fast across the runway, I was pleasantly awed by the sheer immensity of the base. As far as I could see were rows of hangars and revetments protecting camouflaged Phantom jets and C-130 airplanes. Rows of olive drab Huey helicopters sat idle like prehistoric dragonflies with their blades tilted at rest. The constant roar of props and scream of departing fighters accented the hustle and bustle. The base was a veritable beehive of activity giving the impression that the war was in high gear.

Everything seemed to dance and shimmer through endless veils of heat vapors. As we neared the briefing room, I was half blinded by an intense glare. I squinted and shaded my eyes with my hand trying to discern the source. The angle of reflection shifted as I neared the building. That's when I realized what it was. I was shocked to see a fifteen foot wall of reusable caskets stretching the length of a football field. The burnished aluminum had served as a mirror to reflect the sun's rays. The sight was chilling. I remember saying, "Can you believe this man? They must be getting ready for something big." It was an ominous welcome to Vietnam—a morbid reminder of our possible fate. We each passed in solemn review, shaken by the enormous stack of coffins. It gave me the creeps to think my remains could be baking in some zippered bodybag stuffed in one of those boxes.

After our initial in-country processing, we were loaded onto buses with wire screens covering the windows, and taken to a temporary transit barracks to await our Special Forces assignments. Except for some routine check-ins, we were pretty much on our own for the next week. We took full advantage of the liberty.

Saigon was a city of extremes. It still retained a distinctive French flavor from colonial days which manifested itself in the architecture, open air cafes, and second language of the cultured Vietnamese. But there was no escaping the prevailing oriental blends of Indochina. The main streets were lined with stalls and colorful shops selling fruit and vegetables, coke, transistor radios, cigarettes and Kodak film. Sidewalks were cluttered with crippled Vietnamese vets begging for handouts, ARVN soldiers in pegged fatigues, beautiful Vietnamese women wearing the traditional Ao dais or tight jeans and halter tops, short-sleeve businessmen, khaki clad G.I.'s, and Vietnamese police we sarcastically referred to as the "White Mice." The city was a sprawling maze of humanity—from the filthy rich in their fashionable villas to the desperately poor in the squalid shanty towns.

Once we left the gates of our compound, we were thrust into the mainstream of Saigon. The streets were a conjested mass of vehicles and pedestrians. They were filled with pedicabs, bicycles, Jeeps, Lambrettas, trucks, carts and an occasional Citröen all jockeying for preeminence. The raucous sounds of sputtering Vespas, the throaty cough of diesel engines and the honk of impatient horns, underscored our attempts to negotiate the crowded intersections. I was only a novice, but it appeared to me that the sole traffic law was that the biggest vehicle had the right of way. Agile scooters were the only exception. The noxious belch of diesel exhaust, human sweat, and the spicy smells of oriental cooking choked the stagnant air. But the exotic mixture was enticing as much as revolting.

Our first objective was to explore the infamous vices of Saigon. Our primary destination was Tu Do Street—the Vietmanese equivalent of Sodom and Gomorrah. Tu Do was a strip of sensual delights. It was the place where east met west—where American sleaze had left its ugly imprint. It was capitalism at its raunchiest—a place of wall to wall bars and whorehouses and back alley opium dens. It was a mecca for pimping and pandering and profiteering.

Sidewalks were burdened with black market vendors selling goods pilfered from the docks and warehouses, off-duty servicemen, and money changers hustling G.I.'s at the going rate. The singsong chatter of broken English and jabbering Vietnamese in high pitched voices filtered through the crowded sidewalks. Juvenile pimps and ten-year-old con men propositioned Australians and Americans for sex; "Hey G.I., you want boom boom? You come meet my sister. She virgin. Only 12 year old. She beaucoup pretty baby san. Numbah one. Only 500 pee. You see, okay?" Some were motioning servicemen into alleyways to display vulgar porn photos. Others peddled dope; "You want buy happy smoke. Only five dollah a bag." You name it, whores, heroin, opium, Cambodian Black, you could get it. In Tu Do you could indulge in every perversity under the sun if you had the right color of money.

Through shadowy doorways, the blaring sounds of rock music reverberated into the streets. They were the seductive sounds of "Come On Baby Light My Fire," "I Can't Get No Satisfaction," or the electric wail of Jimi Hendrix' guitar screaming, "All Along The Watchtower." The bars had different names—some American, some Vietnamese. But they were all the same dingy dives. They were all staffed by seductive Vietnamese prostitutes in mini-skirts or Ao dais with a long slit up their thighs. They all spoke the same rehearsed lines, "You cute G.I. You buy me drink, okay?" It was the same universal come-on from bargirls who acted like you were their only true love but had no other desire than to run up the bar tab sipping Cokes or Saigon tea before taking you upstairs for a quick trick. They were there to take your money to support their impoverished families or make some Madam or Vietnamese Colonel rich on American dollars.

But for hungry servicemen with money to burn there was little concern where their money ended up if it bought the desired pleasures.

The Vietnamese women were extremely beautiful, especially if they had the exotic mixture of French and Vietnamese. Their skin was a soft amber. Their eyes were almond shaped without the extra oriental fold of skin. Their hair was a silken jet-black which often cascaded to their waists. They were petite and delicate but incredibly sensuous. Americans were only too vulnerable to their enticements, and only too willing to pay for their services.

The farther out in the bush you got, the more ragged the whores and greater the chance of venereal disease. The fear of syphilis and gonorrhea was always in the back of your mind, especially when you heard the Army's horror stories of soldiers catching an incurable strain of black syphilis which was immune to antibiotics. The stories had reached almost folklore proportions. Supposedly, if you caught it, they quarantined you on an island in the South China Sea or sent you to Guam until you died. They notified your parents that you had been killed in action so they could collect the military life insurance policy.

In secured areas, the military took pretty good care of their troops. They tested the prostitutes periodically for VD to make sure they were up on their shots. The whores of Tu Do were generally cleaner and more high class than those out in the bush who had usually lost any semblance of beauty by their early twenties along with most of their teeth. All that was left were cavernous mouths of rotten snags and pomegranate teeth and gums from the constant chewing of betelnuts. A soldier had to be pretty hard up to even consider a few minutes in the grass. But we all degenerated the further out in the bush we went. The swamps and paddy lands of the Mekong Delta provided their own crude brand of pleasures and perversities for desperate men.

We spent a week reveling in a hedonistic paradise during off hours waiting for our transportation to be requisitioned. That's when we were issued our gear. We were issued camouflaged fatigues, flak jackets, helmets, bush hats, and an assortment of jungle necessities like foot powder, insect repellent, and mosquito netting. I must admit, I looked a little rakish in my floppy bush hat; almost like I was preparing for a safari in the outback.

We were also issued weapons. I drew an M-14. I liked the knockdown power but found it too cumbersome. I got rid of it in place of a lighter weight sawed-off version when I got out in the bush. Unlike front line infantry units, we were given a lot of latitude in the individual selection and preference of weapons. The weapons we checked out only went to supplement our personal inventories we had brought over from the states. When we got to our boats, I stayed with the M-60's most of the time. We also used M-16's and Savage 12-gauge shotguns with flechette rounds.

During the days we pulled light duty. My first night in Saigon, I was picked to ride "shotgun" to go to Tan Son Nhut to pick up a busload of new arrivals. They gave me a vintage Thompson submachine gun to give me some clout. I felt like Vic Morrow cruising through the streets to the airport. It was one of those olive drab buses with heavy wire mesh windows so the Vietnamese couldn't toss in garbage or grenades.

I felt real cocky in my camouflaged fatigues and black beret, like I'd been killing Cong in the jungle for months, like I could spit bullets or rip somebody's eyes out of their sockets just for looking at me wrong. And I had only been in 'Nam myself for a few hours. Eyes were riveted on me as I half swaggered into the terminal like John Wayne himself. I walked across the lobby with the butt of the Thompson resting on my hip. I was playing the role to the hilt. I could feel the stares following me and hear the whispers, "Hey, check out that commando; he must be one of those Special Forces dudes." I was eating it up. A few guys tried to ask me questions, but I didn't answer, or simply burned holes through them with my X-ray vision. I was just so bad.

After a few hours of running errands, we hit the night life of Saigon. The first few nights we climbed up to the rooftops of French cafes to watch the nightscape illuminated by the incandescent glare of flares and tracers. We sat in wrought-iron chairs under table umbrellas smoking cigarettes and drinking beers with Vietnamese girls on our laps taking in the bizarre light show. In the distance staccato streaks of green tracers climbed into the blackness like Morse Code, while iridescent red rivers probed the ground from aerial Gatling guns. Occasionally, intermittent orange flashes from artillery rounds punctuated the skyline, followed in seconds by the muffled rumble of distant thunder. The ghoulish light of parachute flares haloed in a greenish glow, cast eerie shadows across the landscape as they spiraled downward dripping phosphorous globs and leaving a distorted corkscrew of smoke in their wake. It was like viewing a lethal light show, but it was off in the distance. We could still fondle giggling Vietnamese bargirls and drink another beer under the safety of our umbrellas. The curtain of the night would be rolled back soon enough, exposing us to the war close up and personal. But for now, we contented ourselves with temporal pleasures, which numbed the senses and helped push the inevitable from our minds.

10

Mekong Headquarters

After a week of killing time in Saigon, my orders came through assigning me and several other new arrivals in our transit barracks to a special boat unit—SEAL Team One in Sa Dec (Com Riv Ron 5), lying about seventy-five miles southwest of Saigon.

A flurry of orders fragmented the group I had been partying with, sending us to Special Forces camps throughout III and IV Corps. It was fun while it lasted but duty called and we had little choice but to obey. After a few crude jibes and lighthearted jests, we patted each other on the backs and said our goodbyes. Most of us would never see each other again.

We loaded our gear onto a deuce-and-a-half truck and wove our way one last time through the conjested streets to Tan Son Nhut Airbase. MACV/SOG had requisitioned a transport to ferry us south. It was one of those flat black Caribous belonging to Air America. The Caribou was a twin prop workhorse used to ferry men and supplies around the country on short hops. We climbed inside the fuselage from a rear ramp and secured our gear.

The heat inside the cargo bay was absolutely stifling. It was cramped with miscellaneous cargo, duffle bags, weapons, nylon safety netting, and five of us including a casual looking crewman with wavy blond hair and aviator glasses who looked like he was privately groovin' on something. Two diesel engines mounted on wooden pallets anchored to the floor by thick chains shared the tight compartment. The fuselage had several small seats along the sides. I took one look at them and decided to climb on top of one of the engines.

When everything was secure, the pilot revved the prop, causing the compact cargo bay to shudder from the vibration. A few minutes later, we bolted down the runway and shot upward into a cobalt blue sky in a steep ascent. We were still climbing when the "ping" of stray small arms fire hit the plane. I was glad I had decided to position several hundred pounds of cast-iron block between me and the waffled flooring.

Because Sa Dec had no airfield, we were shuttled to Vinh Long. Our short flight south took us over the heart of the Mekong Delta. We droned westward crossing and recrossing the tributaries of the Mekong River, snaking out of Southeast Asia before spilling its waste into the South China Sea. I maneuvered around the crowded cargo bay to get an aerial view of the Delta from one of the windows.

The occasional sampan or Vietnamese junk could clearly be seen plying the muddy waters below. At certain angles, sunlight refracted off the mustard colored waterways and water-filled bomb craters like a lattice work of liquid mercury. From horizon to horizon you could see the telltale mosaic of shallow dikes and jade-colored paddy fields. Here and there, jungle smothered outcroppings and mangrove swamps interrupted the broad expanse of alluvial fields, swamps, and yellow-green stands of sawgrass. Occasionally, cloud puffs drifted lazily beneath us casting their shadowy silhouettes across the landscape. The country was deceptively tranquil as we floated westward safely out of range of ground fire.

We touched down on the compacted dirt runway at Vinh Long adjoining an army compound. We were immediately assaulted by the unbearable heat and humidity. A brassy sun high overhead was absolutely punishing in its intensity. The air out in the Delta seemed even more supercharged with moisture than the muggy atmosphere of Saigon. At times, it seemed so choked with water it felt like you were breathing inside a plastic baggie. You couldn't help noticing the rank odor of burning kerosene and crap floating downwind of the compound.

A couple of dusty Jeeps picked us up and delivered us to the nearby army compound. One look at the camp and I knew we were in a war zone. It was a maze of guard towers, sandbagged bunkers, and mortar pits surrounded by miles of coiled concertina wire and moats bristling with needle sharp punji sticks angled outward in a menacing gesture.

It was nearing the end of the hot season when the monsoon rains had long subsided, leaving a blistering sun to torture the land with its unyielding heat. Each year, Vietnam endures a sodden world of driving rains and drizzle. Almost daily, towering blue-black thunderheads massed over the mountains of Cambodia before monsoon winds drove the pregnant cloudbursts toward the sea, releasing torrential sheets of rain. In a few short weeks, I too would suffer the return of the wet season and the discomforts of the deluge. At times, the monsoons rained inches in minutes. Billions of incoming droplets hit the ground like miniature bomb bursts, churning the dirt into a muddy gumbo and causing the river's surface to dance in the downpour. Nothing escaped the near constant drumming—sandbags, bunkers, poncho liners, barbed wire, canvas, men. Relentless lines pelted the corrugated metal roofing until it reached a noisome crescendo which sounded like a thousand snare drums.

But the rains had passed, leaving in their wake rotting canvas, mildew and mold. When the rains subsided and blue skies returned to the Delta, the muddy bog of the military compound had baked fast in the tropical heat. The mud had first turned dry as cardboard and then to an intolerable dust which had, like its rainy counterpart, coated everything with a powdery layer of reddish dust the consistency of fine flour.

Months of private apprehension had weighed heavily upon our minds. There is a certain measure of apprehension associated with life in the slow lane—having a baby, taking a drivers test, or holding a job interview. But, the anxious anticipation of facing combat has few equals. Our anxieties had been mounting for months. It was a pressure within our systems that demanded relief.

Until that moment, ours had been a "wait and see" war of nerves. Months of nagging uncertainties played upon secret forebodings and self-doubts. They were the tormented misgivings of men moving to the front. The waiting had only magnified the gut-gnawing suspense.

We had trained hard, but in spite of extensive preparation, we each instinctively knew there are no certainties in war. It is the grimmest game of chance. Some by prudence, or prowess, or superstition, try to beat the odds. Others would reach the ultimate conclusion birthed by war—the fatalistic resignation that when all is said and done, there's no escaping the bullet with your name on it. When your number's up; it's up. It makes no difference whether you're cringing in the recesses of a bunker, wearing a flak jacket, or pulling point toward a waiting ambush.

We were finally in the thick of it. Reports of ferocious fighting had already preceded our arrival, sufficiently pricking tormented curiosities. It was early summer on the backside of the infamous Tet offensive which had ravaged the length and breadth of South Vietnam. In Saigon, we had heard the horror stories of the street to street fighting in the Cholon District, the overrunning of the American Embassy, the synchronized rocket and mortar attacks, and the fall of the old Imperial City of Hue up north. The Mekong Delta had also suffered its own share of battles.

We asked our black driver, "What's it like here?" and he shrugged with a matter-of-fact indifference, "Hey, my man, rest at ease. A bunch of gooks overran us about a month ago, but don't you know, Mr. Charles got his butt kicked but good." You could see the evidence by the gutted buildings and pockmarked bullet holes in the plastered walls. One of the new guys inquired, "Where's the enemy?"; as if you could point across an imaginary field of battle and see his trenches and company flags fluttering in the breeze. But, this wasn't Sicily, or Shiloh, or the Somme. This was a war without fronts, against an elusive enemy whose only uniform was often no more than Ho Chi Minh sandals and black pajamas. The enemy was probably working behind the bar, sweeping out the hooches, or shaving G.I. necks with straight razors by day in the local barber shop. At night they were planting booby traps or plotting mortar attacks.

I spent the first night in the army compound. Except for a midnight foray into the radio tower to observe the familiar nightscape of illumination flares, chopper running lights, and green tracers, my first Mekong night was uneventful.

The following morning, the same dust-covered Jeeps picked us up and drove us down to the docks to await a couple PBR's who would take us upriver to the Navy Special Forces compound at Sa Dec.

The familiar signature of 220 horsepowered diesel engines caused heads to turn in unison. A couple of PBR's returning from a mission up the Song Tien Giang rounded a bend upstream and pulled into view. They pushed downriver toward us cutting gentle bow sprays with their flared keel. They veered toward us from midstream, with the lead boat aiming for the general direction of the dock. The patrol officer changed the direction of the water jet nozzle to reverse to slow his approach. He maneuvered the helm, then gunned his throttle a couple of times, amplifying the distinctive gurgle sounds of the Jacuzzi water jet propulsion pump. A guy in the forward guntub gave a dumbface smile and flashed an upturned finger in jest at someone on the bank. With his drift under control, the pilot skillfully guided the boat into the mooring slot and shut down the engines. I felt like a preschooler watching his older brothers returning from school even though I'd manned the same boats back in the states.

We had only been sweltering in the river bottom heat for a few minutes when the two PBR's pulled into the dock. It was my first sight of the "Mekong Headhunters." Each of the boats had a skull and crossbones painted on their bows giving the swashbuckling appearance of river pirates. Each of the boats had seen better days. They bore the battle scars of numerous firefights. There were holes and patches all over the boats. Some were nice, neat bullet holes. Others were jagged fist-sized gouges with sharp splintered edges. Peppered scuffs and nicks in the deck, cabin coweling, and fiberglass hull bore silent testimony to B-40 rocket shrapnel. The boats could absorb a lot of abuse, but we all knew that they weren't armor plated tanks. They had their limits, as well as we.

The camouflaged river rats who would be our escorts were a grungy bunch. There was no uniform consistency in their dress code. They wore a rag-tag mix of cutoffs, camouflaged fatigues, boonie hats and black berets. They were an ill-kept lot of half-shaven men who looked like mercenaries from some privately funded army.

We threw our seabags on, then climbed aboard. The helmsman brought the engines to life, swung the boat into mid-channel, then throttled down with the other boat in hot pursuit. We skimmed along the opposite bank going full bore with the second boat riding our outside bow wake. I was a little nervous riding so close to the bank but it didn't seem to phase the old-timers in the least. They were too busy listening to the "oldies but goodies" on the Armed Forces Station in Saigon, or breaking out beers from a cooler load of ice. I thought it was a little strange drinking beers on board, but I soon learned you sweated it out as fast as you poured it in—kind of like being a human sieve. You had to drink quite a few in rapid succession to get drunk.

They may have manifested a rough, almost slovenly appearance, but they were not to be misjudged. They were elite professionals in every sense of the word. My introduction to the team was met with reserved nods and cautious handshakes. There was a certain air of standoffishness underlying my reception. It was not an air of smug indifference, but prudence. They were understandably aloof and leery of the "new guy." I was an unknown, untried in battle, an unpredictable factor in a firefight. Until I proved my metal and drew first blood, I would not be welcomed as a full-fledged river rat.

They were an unorthodox group of rogues who lived hard and played hard. They were nothing short of animals, little more than a pack of mongrels who played by their own rules and took little lip from screw-up officers or tolerated the petty rules of military conformity. They knew how to fight like a coordinated pack of timber wolves, but each was fiercely independent and jealously guarded his right to do as he pleased. They held standard regulations in contempt by dressing according to preference. Some wore tiger greens, some black pajamas, others fatigue cutoffs. All in all, it was a defiant reflection of their "who cares, don't even mess with me" attitude. With my predisposition, I would find it easy to assimilate into their wacko brand of nonconformity.

Several hours later, we banked left into an intersecting canal. We sailed under a narrow bridge and cruised past a collection of hooches perched on stilts. The banks were lined with children, old men sitting on their haunches

Vietnamese style, and occasional ARNV soldiers. We continued on until we passed an army compound, then pulled into a navy pier where a small flotilla of PBR's, SEAL Team Assault Boats, and a repair barge were tied up.

A couple more Jeeps carried us about a mile and a half to our compound. The driver put the peddle to the metal as he careened through town like a Tokyo cab driver. We rushed past open air shops peddling fish, produce, woven baskets and cloth and soup stalls selling Fa and Soup Chinoise. The rotten fish smell of Nouc-Mam permeated the marketplace. Even out in the Delta, the influence of French Colonialism was very much present in the architecture.

Our navy compound had the typical appearance of concertina wire, sandbag bunkers, and guard towers. Across from us was an R.O.K. compound which was somewhat comforting even to Navy SEALS. The Viet Cong were terrified of the South Koreans because the Koreans were vicious soldiers who gave the communists no slack. They were all crack soldiers skilled in guerrilla warfare and the martial arts.

Our compound was a collection of navy personnel, Seabees, and Special Forces teams. Within our barbed wire enclosure were administrative buildings, barracks, an EM Club, showers, latrines, and a chow hall. We were a self-contained compound of barracks, bunkers, and bars.

I reported in and was shown to my barracks where I was issued a cot and given a locker to store my gear. My C.O. seemed like an all right sort of guy with a fatherly, almost protective, nature. Unlike some jerk XO's under him, which I would come to despise and seriously contemplate fragging, he was one of the few good officers I had the honor to serve under. He assigned me to Special Boat Unit 524, comprised of the standard five team patrols of two PBR's each. We were a unique unit of the brown water navy. The Special Boat Unit 524, operating under the covert auspices of S.O.G. carried out some missions that were so top-secret, we were later known as "the unit that never was."

I spent the first couple of days getting outfitted in preparation for my upcoming missions with the Mekong River Rats. I selected tiger greens and a camouflaged bush hat which we sarcastically referred to as "go to hell hats." We called them that because if you ever took a round through it, that's where you would end up. The traditional steel pot offered more protection, but the guys in our outfit felt that only "pansies" wore them. I didn't have much use for the cumbersome flak jackets either. They were too uncomfortable and hot. The only standard piece of protection I wore was the American issue jungle boots with their canvas sidings, mesh-vented portholes for quick drying and protective steel shank which offered some protection against dung-dipped punji sticks.

Within days, I was thrust into Riverene duty under the watchful tutelage of my more seasoned shipmates. The long nagging uncertainty of how I would respond under fire was soon resolved. My "baptism of fire" was eased by the support of my fellow river rats who had weathered the same uncertainties themselves and prevailed. The encouragement of the camp corpsman, who gave me a much needed boost of confidence, was especially helpful. I remember probing him in not so subtle ways; "Have you ever come across guys cracking up or losing it in a firefight"; it was kinda like asking someone a personal question about a hypothetical situation involving someone else when you didn't want them to know you were talking about yourself. "I know this guy who has a friend who talked to someone else about this guy they know who was in a firefight . . . ," that sort of thing. But he was no fool. He saw right through me and, in his own understanding way, got a sympathetic smile on his face and said, "Hey man, you got plenty of training. You made it this far. When the time comes down, you will do what is right." All I could say was "thanks." Time would prove him right.

As members of Naval Intelligence Special Operations Group attached to SEAL Team One, our Riverene Section ran the gamut of covert activities ranging from assassinations and kidnapping of V.C. leaders and political cadre under the highly effective "Pheonix Program," to clandestine insertions and retrievals of SEAL Team commando units. We also carried out a variety of reconnaissance missions, night ambushes, and patrols along the muddy brown tributaries and canals which dissected the Mekong Delta. For several months we were attached to the U.S. Army 5th Special Forces at Chau Doc operating under MACV/SOG along the Cambodian border.

Ours was a cunning game of stealth, hunting humans, the most elusive and cunning of prey. We were hunting animals who often hunted you in return. The watery world of the paddy lands and backwater swamps were our habitat. The jungle outcroppings were our territorial hunting grounds, and unlike most American ground units who relinquished the countryside back to Charlie after their daily 9 to 5 war, we were nocturnal creatures who hunted mainly at night.

The Mekong nights had many faces. Many an apprehensive night was spent in ominous solitude mid-river or drifting silently with the current. There were vulnerable nights lurking at the entrance of a narrow canal or river bend waiting for Charlie to appear. There were oppressive nights beached at the river's edge, overgrown with jungle so thick it rose from the water's edge like a lush green wall, jungle so congested it could swallow a man in a couple of paces—nights of anxious anticipation enduring the insufferable puffs of mosquitos which batted about our heads in a relentless quest for blood while we waited for a firefight which would never come.

There were nights so dark there was barely enough light from a scudding overcast to illuminate our Starlight Scopes. There were eerie, brooding nights faintly illuminated by a pallow tint of moonlight—quiet nights when the luminous outline of clouds drifted beneath a full moon—distant nights of endless stars. Some nights were as quiet as a grave. Others were serenaded by an exotic symphony of insects, monkeys, frogs, and jungle birds.

Most were long and tedious nights which weighed heavily upon us—clammy, restless, waiting nights with rounds chambered and fingers impatiently caressing triggers. But there were also sudden moments of high intensity terror, when flashbulb explosions rent the curtain of blackness and phosphorous tracers slashed lethal lines over the screams of youthful men.

11

F-Troop

The men of the 524th Riverene Section kept to themselves, intimidating outsiders by their renegade reputation. Most officers gave us a wide berth, especially the pencil pushing types. I think the navy wanted it that way. We were a bit of an embarrassment even if we were a necessary evil—kind of like a junkyard dog which serves a useful purpose but you don't want to bring it out to play with kids or paw visitors. Reporters from *Stars and Stripes* or the major wire services would come by in their Jeeps every so often, sniffing out a good story, but we steered clear of them. We knew they were real jerks who were either looking for brainless stories on the lighter side or dirt. Besides, we didn't want any of the more persistent types getting wind of our activities.

We also avoided the CIA nerds from Saigon and the computer whizzes from the Rand Corporation. They were supposedly waging a sophisticated, state-of-the-art war using computers and electronic sensing devices dropped by aircraft. They'd calculate troop movements and enemy concentrations based upon their intelligence and statistical projections. But their conclusions usually got us into a world of hurt. They'd inform us that an insertion point would be safe. We would find it crawling with V.C. Their high-tech brainstorming backfired half of the time and only fueled our contempt for higher-ups, whether in uniform or not.

As part of the 524th Special Boat Unit, I was assigned to "F" troop, "Fox Trot Patrol." We were one of the most unruly rag-tag "who cares," "don't give a damn," "hell bent for leather" band of maniacs in the Mekong. And "F" troop was the meanest group of perpetual screwups in our entire contingent. Two of the guys in our troop were the only Americans I knew in the history of the Vietnam War to have actually been thrown out of the country. They went on a berserk rampage at three o'clock one morning and shot up a local whorehouse which was also servicing NVA on R&R, rearranging several V.C. prostitutes and totally destroying the building. It was an embarrassing incident for MACV headquarters who sought to brush the affair under the carpet by unceremoniously deporting them back to the states.

Though outsiders were viewed with suspicion and shunned within our inner circle of teenage sociopaths, we formed some pretty tight bonds within the section, especially with our immediate crewmates. I spent a lot of my time up in the bow guntub. I got a kick out of cruising full throttle down a jungle lined canal behind a set of twin 50's wearing sunglasses and letting the wind blow through my hair, sipping "33 Beer" and singing "Satisfaction" by the "Stones." Each of us relished the roles we played and the sense of kinship we felt. It was a total head trip.

In spite of our independence, we all instinctively recognized the need for one another. It was one of the last tokens of humanity we had left. In spite of our sarcastic jibes and combat cynicism, we cherished our brotherhood more deeply than any of us were willing to admit. We may have clowned around a lot, flaunted our breakdown of

conventional discipline, and had too many liquid break-
fasts after night patrols, but when it came to combat, we
played our roles with deadly seriousness. There was little
room for carelessness out in the bush.

One of the guys I was paired with was Bernie Fletcher.
Bernie was one of those half comical looking guys who
just didn't look like he belonged in the Special Forces, let
alone a war zone. He was a short and wiry little guy who
bore a remarkable resemblance to Alfred E. Newman.
With his wire, chrome-tinted glasses and floppy bush hat,
he seemed deceptively out of place. Oddly enough, some
guys who never quite seem to fit back in the world found
a perfect haven in Vietnam. Bernie had not only adapted
to the Mekong madness, but had actually thrived. He had
already completed two full tours and re-upped for a third.
Bernie was always squatting on his haunches like the Vietnamese. He had been incountry so long he could chatter
away in Vietnamese better than most of the locals. He was
also a real party animal who, despite his awkward appearance, could out party some of the wildest guys in the
outfit.

Several months into my first tour, Bernie's dad manipulated a visit to our compound. He was a civilian contrac-
tor working for the U.S. government. When his old man
showed up, it wasn't hard to see where Bernie got his
crazies. Like father, like son. Even we had a hard time
chaperoning the guy. We literally chased his dad all over
Sa Dec, from one bar and brothel to the next.

We thought we'd liven up his visit a bit by sneaking him
out on patrol with us, loaded down with a cooler full of
ice and a couple cases of beer. We thought it would be an
interesting side trip for Bernie's dad—like living in L.A.
and taking a visiting uncle from Kansas to see Disneyland.
We didn't think anything would happen, just a few beers
and a starlit cruise down the Mekong. But we ran into a
brief but electrifying firefight that nearly gave his dad a
heart attack. When it was over, we were cracking up while

his dad was curled up in the corner of the boat as white as a sheet. He thought we were nuts. All he could say was, "My God, you guys are out of your friggin minds." That was the first and only time he went out with us. For the rest of his visit, he stuck close to the bars. I don't think his dad left quite the same.

Whenever we pulled into the Provincial Capitol of My Tho downriver to grab a few beers or make a quick stop at one of the local brothels, you would have thought a national folk hero had returned home. Bernie's fame was almost legendary. It was like a family reunion. News of Bernie's return seemed to spread through the red light district like a prairie fire. A couple dozen prostitutes came out of the woodwork and flocked around Bernie like rats around the Pied Piper. They just hung on him and giggled like infatuated schoolgirls. Bernie just flashed a gloating grin and ate up the adoration while the girls chortled, "Fletcher, Fletcher, Fletcher." Probably half of the one-year-olds in the town belonged to Bernie. If they'd held an election for mayor, he would have been elected on the spot.

The first night with the 524th, I sat in the navy bar in Sa Dec next to Bernie. He was drinking "Salty Dogs." It was just about last call that night and the remaining bar crowd was feeling no pain. Bernie slurred to the bartender, "Give me seventeen salties to go." The bartender filled the glasses one by one and set them back to back on the bar. The idea was to try to drink each other under the table. If you passed out, they dragged you out of the bar and left you crumpled outside the door in the dirt. It was a machismo test of endurance to see who could hold their booze the best.

Well, obviously, Bernie had been practicing for two years and usually won. We took turns chugalugging the drinks one by one, burping and belching in a glassy-eyed stupor. Our bladders were about to burst as we kept pouring liquid in with nothing coming out. The restroom was a crude affair. It was a 55-gallon drum buried in the ground with the bottom drilled out and a wire screen over the top. You stood over it, doing a precarious balancing act, and swished into the drum. Some drinking bouts got so raucous that nobody bothered stumbling to the latrine, they just positioned themselves in the doorway and urinated on the pile of losers. I guess I proved I was worth something that night as a new guy because I didn't pass out or vomit all over myself, although I had to be helped back to the barracks.

Another one of my teammates was Ryan Bittner from Boston. He was lean and sinewy and sported a Fu Man Chu moustache. He had dark, scheming eyes which always looked like they were privy to some devious joke. The rest of the crew affectionately nicknamed him "The Mule." He was a total animal, wacked out from too many tours in 'Nam. He and Bernie went way back. Being in 'Nam could have the same debilitating effect as a degenerative disease. Both were showing advanced symptoms. When I was first introduced to Ryan, he motioned me over to his locker with a mischievous grin. "Man, I want you to check out my girlfriend." He opened his locker door, and on the back side was a large poster of a naked black woman about nine months pregnant squatting on some tenement steps. He was definitely strange. I remember thinking at the time that his gears must be grinding. But he was just trying to blow my mind.

The final crewmate was Buddy Mercer. He was compact and muscular with sun bleached hair and a deep tan from months on the river. He hailed from New Hampshire, but looked more like a Malibu surfer. Buddy was a born comedian, a total sanguine, who always had a humorous comeback. Buddy was a running commentary of one-liners and witty observations, which in some strange way added a touch of sense to our daily insanity. Whenever something went wrong, Buddy's famous epitaph lightened the mood, "What a bummer!" He was our private version of the U.S.O. and added a lighter note of comic relief to the more sinister sides of our environment.

Buddy wasn't the animal the rest of us were. He was more gentle by nature and seemed to take life in stride. Oh, he definitely got off on the high intensity rush of a firefight, but he was not into violence for violence sake. Buddy was more into mind games and getting it on. Of all the crew members, me and Buddy formed the closest alliance. We grew to be closer than brothers. In fact, it got to the point that someone would be looking for one of us and say, "Hey Buddy," or "Hey Mickey, where's your brother?"

One of our big things was to imitate the characters of the old "Buster Brown Show" we had each grown up with as kids. That was in itself a subtle commentary on the youthful trappings of the boy soldiers of 'Nam. After all, we'd grown up with Buster Brown, the Mouseketeers, and Captain Kangaroo. There was this cat named Midnight, a little mouse with a squeaky voice, and of course a magic frog named "Froggie" who had a deep throaty voice. We imitated the voices back and forth in our private little world like six-year-olds lost in a backyard sandbox with their Tonka trucks.

The four of us formed a depth of camaraderie and friendship seldom rivaled back in the states. There was almost nothing we wouldn't have done for one another, whether that meant sharing your last cigarette or letter from home, or laying down your life in a firefight to save one another. They were relationships of self-sacrificing love and loyalty which, even in the bloodletting of 'Nam, embodied the highest virtues in humanity. They were relationships seldom forged outside the rarefied atmosphere of combat, relationships many had never experienced before and few since. Ours was an intimacy of understanding that still lingers today, though we only endured a few passing months of brotherhood on a battlefield half a world away.

In the navy bar at Sa Dec, we had an initiation. We had

green Gecko lizards in 'Nam with long narrow tails. They were always clinging to the walls or screens. To pass the initiation you had to grab one of the lizards by the tail and swallow him alive without biting him. You were only permitted to wash him down with beer. Most of the contestants would gag and heave their guts out. If you could keep the lizard down, while it fought for its life inside your stomach, you were cool.

The local whorehouses were euphemistically referred to as the "barber shop." In fact, a number of them were on the upper floor with a barber shop downstairs serving as a store front. Special Boat Unit 524 had become celebrities among the local prostitutes. They thought we were a bunch of "cowboys." All of the G.I.'s who frequented the pleasure dens of Sa Dec let down their hair somewhat. But they were tame in comparison to our wildness. Even the seedy life of prostitution could grow routine for the ranks of swing-shift whores. We added a little spice to their drudgery.

During one of our off-duty drinking bouts, one of the guys was reminiscing about the good times and came up with an idea to make a film about our exploits. It was a pretty amateurish Super 8 production with jerky shots and adolescent antics. We came up with a real original title. We called it "The Good, The Bad, and The Ugly." Buddy was the Good, I was the Bad, and Ryan "The Mule" was the Ugly, although it was a toss-up between him and Bernie. It was a stupid flick with clips of us chasing up and down the river acting like P.T. 109 or goofing around drinking beer and making faces in the camera.

We really got into a couple of perverted takes of battlefield comedy. A couple of scenes in particular showcased the sociopathic level we had sunk to. For supporting roles, we incorporated some V.C. body parts from a firefight. In one scene, the camera was following a pair of weathered jungle boots down a trail. As the suspense mounted, the camera slowly made its way up the legs of the soldier brushing past vegetation. The figure gave the impression of pursuing something, as it ran deeper into the jungle. The camera climbed the torso exposing a K-bar, grenades, and bandoliers of machine gun ammo. Then the camera suddenly scanned upward exposing two heads on the soldier's shoulders. It was Ryan running down the trail while balancing the decapitated head of some V.C. next to his own. Then for a ghoulish finale, he turned, kissed the guy on the cheek and looked back into the camera with a sly grin and gave a prankish wink.

In another scene, we planned to shock the crew members of one of the floating resupply barges moored mid-river in the Mekong. The guys stationed on board had the air conditioned comforts of a rear area. We knew some of them, especially some of the glory boy officers who wrote G.I. Joe letters to their girlfriends back home bragging about how tough it was while they relaxed in air conditioned comfort, watching movies and filling out reports. We figured we'd gross them out with a taste of the real thing.

Our PBR's had two antenna on board. So we took two arms that had been severed just below the elbows and skewered them on the ends of the antenna, which gave the macabre impression they were waving. Then we waited for the appropriate timing to pull our stunt.

Each morning after breakfast, they would sound quarters for the men to assemble on the decks. They would be standing at attention for roll call while they listened to the Union Jack piped over the ship's intercom. We timed our entrance perfectly and passed by with the severed hands waving at the crew members as they stood in gaped mouth surprise. It was our special after breakfast treat. It was a taste of war they didn't expect to write home about.

We did a lot of idiotic things to relieve the tension. One time Bernie dressed up in his tiger greens with a helmet. He strung belts of .50 caliber ammunition around his shoulders Poncho Villa style. He had fragmentation grenades and smoke canisters pinned all over his chest and was cradling an M-60 machine gun like Rambo. He had a picture taken and sent it to a company back in the states who made personalized greeting cards. He ordered a couple boxes of Christmas cards with "Peace on Earth" underneath the photo. He cynically signed it, "maybe next year."

A lot of men got so fed up with Vietnam that they wrote to their Congressmen and Senators complaining about the halt of bombing raids up north. It only encouraged the North Vietnamese to flood the south with more men and materials. Others bitterly complained about the futility of taking a V.C. stronghold at the cost of American lives only to turn around and let Charlie reclaim it. Others mocked mindless rules of engagement which designated "free-fire-zones" versus a "don't shoot at unless shot at" policy. Such policies posed an insane dilemma for men who were hazarding their lives each day in endless fields of fire. They were letters from embittered men who felt like they were risking their lives fighting a war with one hand tied behind their backs.

Well, unbeknownst to us, Bernie sent one of his personalized cards to President Nixon. We were out on patrol one afternoon when we got a coded message from headquarters to return to base at once. When we got back to our compound, our worried C.O. handed us a letter from the White House embossed with the presidential seal. It was a form letter from the President and his family thanking us for the Christmas card and expressing their hopes that there would be peace on earth next year. It was just another bizarre piece of trivia which underscored the absurdity of our predicament.

Looking back, if it hadn't been for my misfit fraternity of malcontents, I don't think I would have made it at all.

12

Brothers

Not all of our relationships were so warm or enduring. My camaraderie with my crewmates was one thing; my running feud with the officers was another. The seething contempt we felt for egotistical officers dogged us with the relentlessness of the Vietnamese sun.

We became progressively more disenchanted with the state of affairs we had to deal with each day. We were especially bitter at a system which seemed so indifferent to our welfare.

On one operation, our section was assigned to serve as a blocking force for a search and destroy operation the 9th Infantry Division was pulling in the Delta. It was a classic "hammer and anvil" tactic with us beached along a length of canal while the 9th worked their way toward us overland in an attempt to flush the enemy. We had just taken up position along another stagnant slough when men aboard our PBR's started coughing and sneezing uncontrollably. I remember asking Buddy, "Say, what is this?" Within minutes our eyes were burning and our bodies were breaking out with hives and rashes. A couple of men appeared to be having severe allergic reactions. At first, we thought it might be C-S riot gas drifting downwind toward us. Only later did we learn that it was something called ''Agent Orange'' sprayed earlier by a flotilla of C-130's. Our command knew that they were sending us into an area that had just been saturated with one of the most toxic substances known to man—a chemical defoliant which would take the lives of countless Veterans and their offspring years after Vietnam was only a painful memory.

When Nixon ordered a bombing halt up north, the Ho Chi Minh trail turned into an expressway overnight. The North Vietnamese took full advantage of the lull in the bombing to rush supplies south by truck, cart, bicycle, and even human mules. Thousands of well-equipped North Vietnamese regulars poured into the south, resulting in many American casualties. But there was little we could do about it. We all felt victimized by the higher ups.

We'd go out on missions and uncover huge caches of weapons and supplies. There would be tons of American equipment: boots, uniforms, even M-16's. Most of it was black market contraband that had been stolen by the South Vietnamese and sold to the Viet Cong. We would also find medical supplies which had been donated by church groups, SDS groups, left-wing groups, even the Red Cross. Here we were, fighting a war only to discover that fellow countrymen back home were giving aid and comfort to the enemy. It made for some very bitter men. Hundreds of guys grew so disillusioned, they just gave up on the war and walked away. Many went A.W.O.L. and lost themselves in the back alleys of Saigon.

Sometimes it was hard to tell who the enemy really was. On Thanksgiving, we were told that someone had shipped some turkeys to us with all the trimmings. We were informed that we were going to have a real feast, but we had to go out on a search and destroy mission first. We were drooling all night long in anticipation of roasted turkey. But the officers were playing political games with some Air Force officers they had invited over in our absence. We got back that morning only to discover that they had picked the turkeys cleaner than a school of piranha. Such was the distaste we harbored for those over us.

Our C.O. was an Annapolis graduate and a man of integrity. He was a man's man who earned our respect, maybe because we knew that he would never have asked us to do something he would not have been willing to do himself. But he was an exception rather than the rule.

Several of his executive officers under him were self-serving glory boys with inflated egos who cared more for promotions than our welfare. All they seemed to be concerned with was exaggerated body counts. We were expendables. Our fate in the fortunes of war was of little concern if it resulted in higher proportional kill ratios which boosted their efficiency reports and chances for movement up the military ladder.

But the biggest conniver of them all was a Lt. J.G. named Brothers. He was your classic military jerk. He always played it safe. The only times he would go out with us was on relatively safe missions when half the brown water navy was escorting him. He only left his desk when he had to, to chalk up enough missions time to earn his Combat Action Ribbon. We saw more action off duty in the base bar than he did out on patrol. Brothers was a self-serving careerist. He was a consummate apple-polisher who strove to ingratiate himself with our C.O. with such sickening regularity that we got so we couldn't stand the sight of him. He was the ambitious sort of manipulator who would sell out his mother if it would get him a promotion. Men like Brothers were only a daily reminder of a whole chain of command who cared next to nothing for the sacrifices we were making.

When I signed up for a second tour, he came up to me with a pompous air of superiority and told me I was a fool for doing it. I stuck my face in his and responded, ''Yeh, I may be a total fool, Brothers, sir, but at least I'm not a slimeball like somebody we know who decided not to meet his wife in Hawaii for R and R so he could cheat on her in Sydney!''

Brothers was a river rat in name only. He was a bureaucratic part of Special Operations. His primary job was to pass down the orders which came from Naval Intelligence Special Operations headquarters in Saigon. He seldom accompanied us on missions. When he did, we kept a close eye on him so he didn't do something stupid and get us blown away.

The animosity between him and our section was seldom far from our minds. He hated the fact that we were so fiercely independent and outright contemptuous of his authority. There was a constant power play between us. He was far too absorbed with his self-importance. We always suspected he assigned us to some of our dirtier missions in the hopes we wouldn't come back. I'm sure he struggled to conceal his fear of us under the bluster of rank and verbal threats, but he knew he could only push us so far before he'd get "accidently" wasted.

One time Brothers ordered us out on a mission deep into a gridwork of jungle clogged canals. We were stretching our fuel reserves to the limits. We knew we didn't have enough diesel to make it back, but he said they'd resupply us before dark. The fuel gauge kept dropping until the diesels coughed a few times then conked out. Here we were, out in the middle of V.C. infested territory, at the mercy of the current. Without any fuel, we were unable to escape if Charlie hit us from the treeline overhanging the canal. Night was coming on fast and we were getting freaked. Ryan kept radioing in for fuel, but Brothers was stalling. We knew it was a power play on his part to show us who was in charge.

Everyone on board was getting furious. It was like Brothers was setting us up. Ryan coded in a distress call demanding Brothers to send out some boats and pull us out before we got hit. We didn't mind fighting Charlie on equal terms, but not on his. The jungle belonged to him, and without mobility, we were little more than sitting ducks. Brothers waited until the darkness closed in before the boats finally arrived to pull us out.

Brothers was always pulling rank and trying to come down on us. His petty conceit knew no limits as far as subordinates were concerned. If we didn't concede to his superiority he was determined to put us in our place even if he had to get us court-martialed. Well, we gave him plenty of opportunity for that, although we always managed to outwit him. It was somewhat like Hogan's Heroes outsmarting Colonel Klink.

One afternoon, we were on another two boat patrol down some backwater slough. We were screaming down the canal with the second boat riding our bow wake. We were skimming only a few feet from the muddy beach with the second boat on the outside wake when we rounded a bend in the canal. Without warning, we charged around the bend right into the path of several huge poles impaled in the river bottom. They were fishing supports which the Locals used to attach their fishing nets to. To an onrushing boat, they were little more than river punji sticks. Instead of piercing the boot of a hapless soldier, they were about to rip open the hull of our PBR with the ease of a can opener on a tin of sardines.

Ryan swung the helm violently to the left in a desperate attempt to miss the poles but our maneuver sent the trailing PBR crashing into our broadside. I had been sitting up on the bow with a beer sunning myself when Ryan threw us into the violent turn. Before I knew it, I was catapulted off the boat about twenty feet before I plowed into the river. One guy on the other PBR slammed his head into the forward gun turret, splitting it like a watermelon and a second crewmember's face was rearranged by the impact.

It had been a routine patrol with little chance of contact, so we had been partying down on the boat. Crumpled beer cans were strewn all over the deck. Both boats were totaled for the time being. Ours had a yawning hole in the side and the other's bow was a splintered mess of fiberglass. We cleaned up the boats as best we could and tossed the beer cans overboard. After we tidied up the boats, we radioed in that we'd had an accident and needed help. Our boat was taking on water and slowly sinking, so we had to have a couple boats come out and tow us back to the repair barge at Sa Dec. We knew Brothers was beside himself with glee over this one. He had us dead to rights. We'd put two $70,000 boats out of commission and lost some weapons overboard in the impact.

Well, we limped back to Sa Dec to face Brothers. Predictably, he was standing on the pier gloating with that "Boy, I've got you this time" look on his face and his hands cocked on his hips in smug contempt.

Each of us was interrogated separately to find out if our stories jibed. We had been partying down pretty good and had worked our way through a couple cases of beer before we got back. It only encouraged our flippant "beat the system" attitude. When Brothers called me in, he glowered at me in utter disgust, like I was a worthless piece of garbage. "Block, your rear's in a sling. There's no way you and your mongrel crew is going to worm your way out of this one." He shook his head in a mock parody of disbelief.

But we had the last laugh. Before he could proceed, I shot back with the feigned sincerity of Eddy Haskel on "Leave It To Beaver," "Sir, the first thing that I want to go on record is that I want to nominate my friend Ryan Bittner for the Congressional Medal of Honor. Sir, he saved my life when I was thrown over the side. Not only did he react in time to save our crew from hitting those fishing stakes, but he rescued me when the second boat came over the top of me. When I got thrown clear, the water was only a few feet deep so I had to hug the bottom just to keep from getting hit by the PBR. I nearly drowned, but Ryan jumped overboard and dragged me out just in time. Why I'm alive at all is beyond me, but I wouldn't have made it if it hadn't been for his quick thinking."

My request caught Brothers totally off guard. All he could say was, "But, you weren't hit by the boat?" "No sir, but Mule, I mean Ryan, pulled me out before I drowned. I was pretty dazed, sir. So I want to nominate him for the medal."

Brothers was really rattled. I'd got the better of him and we both knew it. "No way, Block! Are you really telling me this, or are you pulling another one of your cute stunts?" I responded with a feigned show of wounded indignation; "Sir, isn't it my right to recommend someone for the Medal of Honor when he went above and beyond the call of duty to save my skin? If you don't let me, I will write my Congressman, my Senator, and the President." I had him by the sling now. Officers like Brothers feared the political flak of a probing Congressman more than Charlie. Brothers was livid. He was so mad his face was almost purple. He was screaming and cursing in absolute frustration. All they ended up doing was chewing us out and telling us never to do it again.

We left the interrogation to celebrate at the nearest bar while Brothers stewed in his rage, determined to get us if it was the last thing he did. But he wasn't the only one determined to win this war.

A few nights later, I found Ryan sitting on his bunk in a sullen mood slipping bullets into a magazine. There was an AK-47 lying on the cot beside him. I knew by the expression on his face that something was up. "What are you going to do, Mule?" He looked at me with a blank look on his face and said, "What do you think I'm going to do? I'm going to waste Brothers." He went back to shoving rounds in the magazine and added, "That jerk has been pushing me for too long. I've had it. I'm going to blow his butt away." All I could say was, "Com'on man, there ain't no way you're going to get away with it.

Everybody's going to know it was you." But I wasn't that persuasive. I wanted Brothers as much as Ryan. "Listen Mule, I've got a plan. Tonight is my night off the boat."

When we were pulling night ambushes, we usually beached along the muddy jungle sloughs. We tied the boats to the shore with ropes and grappling hooks anchored to exposed roots sticking out of the bank. If we had to push off in a hurry, we would simply cut the mooring lines with a machete. So we never beached the boats too high up on the muddy flats in case the tides went out and left us stranded in the muck. When we beached our PBR for a night assault three guys would man the onboard weapons and radio while the fourth guy would set up an LP about 100 yards inland. We took turns pulling the anchor position.

I sat down on the cot across from Ryan and said, "I'll keep watch for a couple of hours in the jungle. You make sure Brothers is on the bow of the boat. Just play it cool and don't act suspicious. We've got to make it look like an ambush. I'll sneak back and blow him away, then throw a couple fragmentation grenades into the bush and start screaming. You will cut loose with everything you've got. We'll radio in and tell the base we got hit. We'll tell them Brothers got killed in the ambush. No one will know the difference. All we've got to do is stand by the story." Ryan tried arguing with me, but after a few minutes he calmed down and agreed to do it my way. Why should he spend his life in Leavenworth when he could get Brothers for free? Besides, it would really make my day!

But by a twist of fate, our plan fell apart at the last minute. Brothers came swaggering down the pier as we were making preparations to shove off. He was wearing polished jungle boots, pressed fatigues and carrying a mint condition M-16. He took one look at us and scowled, with a "you dirty scumbags" look. His eyes shifted suspiciously between our boat and our backup and decided to ride with the other crew.

We pushed upstream through a maze of adjoining canals to a prearranged ambush site. Brothers took his boat about a quarter of a mile up the canal from ours. Our PBR's could run in as little as a few inches of water because of their Jacuzzi pumps which sucked water in and shot it out through nozzles for propulsion. But with the inland ebb tides, we had to be careful not to get grounded on a mud-flat in the outgoing tide. Well, the crew members kept telling Brothers to back the boat off the shore or they were going to get stranded. But he was so pig-headed sure of himself he kept telling them, "No, we're going to stay put until we get some V.C." Well, the tide obeyed the laws of nature and left their boat high and dry. So about three in the morning we get a "break squelch, break squelch" on the radio and a distress call that they were high and dry and wanted us to come and pull them off the muck. We never took Brothers out on another mission with us.

I placed him at the top of my contempt list after a par-ticularly bloody ambush that cost us two boats and their crews. I'll never forget the galling sight of him standing above us with a Kodak Instamatic clicking snapshots with the zeal of a Japanese tourist. He was walking back and forth on the pier snapping pictures of the butchered re-mains of our team members so he could write home and tell his friends how rough it had been. It was a blatant act of desecration for our fallen teammates. Ryan and Bernie came very close to blowing him away on the spot.

Sa Dec's whorehouses had not only serviced the Amer-ican units stationed nearby, but they doubled as an R and R center for a crack regiment of North Vietnamese regu-lars who were operating in the Mekong Delta. It was one thing to fight them out in the jungle, but they hated us controlling their R and R center. They were just looking for the opportunity to strike back. These guys were not peasant farmers running around in tire tread sandals and coolie hats, carrying vintage French rifles. They were highly disciplined soldiers, well-armed with Soviet assault rifles, machine guns, and mortars.

Another two boat patrol had been sent into a notorious labyrinth of canals we referred to as "The Devil's Hole." It was a track of compacted jungle, stagnant sloughs and chest high stands of razor sharp sawgrass. It was also infested with the enemy.

Events had been moving for weeks toward a violent conclusion. The NVA were itching for a fight. We had been sending in psy-op units to harass the enemy with Vietnamese interpreters who shouted every degrading put down they could think of through loud speakers to flush Charlie out of his hiding so we could engage them. But they were waiting to hit us on their own terms, in their own time.

They had deployed a company of 120 NVA in a rough L-shaped ambush around a narrow bend in one of the canals. The lead boat was a PBR and the second was a more heavily armored monitor. When the lead PBR dog-legged left, they let it pass to funnel it deeper into the trap. But when the monitor swung into the bend, the NVA opened up at point blank range with a deadly cacophony of AK's, .51 caliber machine guns, RPG's, and B-40 rockets. They blew the boat to pieces. The guys on board were literally chopped to shreds from the maelstrom of bullets and shrapnel. They didn't have a chance.

The first boat turned and raced back through a gauntlet of machine gun geysers but got hit hard in the process. Only two guys limped out of the ambush. They gunned their bullet-ridden PBR and raced out of the "Devil's Hole" for the safety of a Vietnamese outpost where they radioed in for backup. The South Vietnamese Army knew the place was crawling with NVA but they didn't want to disturb the fragile status quo they had established with the enemy. To them, it was "live and let live." Apart from a few crack South Vietnamese Ranger and Special Forces units, the only thing the ARVN's did well was avoid combat and leave the dirty work to the Americans.

When we got word that our fellow teammates were getting butchered a few miles away, we rushed to our PBR's with the speed of B-52 pilots rushing to their fueled bombers under the emergency scream of Klaxons.

Eight PBR's pulled out loaded to the gunwales with killing power. I'll never forget the sight of Bernie holding his vintage .45 caliber grease gun, looking like he could chew raw meat. The rage etched in his camouflaged face epitomized the feeling of all of us. Ryan pulled out all the stops and raced our dual diesels at full RPM down the jungle-lined canal. We knew one of our boats was in the "Devil's Hole," but we didn't know if some of the crew members were still fighting for their lives.

We were nearly beside ourselves in our frenzy to reach them before it was too late. Our adrenals were working overtime. Some guys were gritting their teeth in grim determination, some were staring down river in silence, others were fidgeting with their weapons with the nervous anticipation of racehorses before the bell. We all knew it could be us who had stumbled into the ambush. Such was the unpredictability of war. In fact, two of the guys were friends. Just the night before, one of them had given Bernie his St. Christopher medal for protection. He said he wouldn't be needing it any longer. What was even more disconcerting was the knowledge that our crew had been scheduled to be on that mission but had been substituted by another boat at the last minute. They were now in the killing zone in our place.

Off in the distance, we could hear sporadic firing. Charlie was making sure no one got out alive. Navy Seawolf choppers had arrived on the scene. They were outlined above the horizon, buzzing the battlefield like angry wasps firing rockets into the jungle.

I was in the forward .50 guntub when we screamed into the ambush site. Everyone onboard the PBR's were firing into the shoreline. Bullets cracked overhead like countless bullwhips. Stray rounds kicked up muddy geysers around our boats or thudded harmlessly into the fiberglass hulls. The ominous *"sssssss zzzzzz whoooo"* of an incoming RPG arced out of the jungle fringe, barely missing one of the boats. An enormous plume of water erupted, showering the PBR in sheets of river water. Inland, deadly blossoms of gray-black smoke burst through the sawgrass from the Seawolf's rocket pods.

Only scattered NVA were still firing from the jungle-covered banks. Most had fled into their jungle sanctuary. The enemy could be as elusive as quicksilver, but this time, we had responded fast enough to cut off some of their retreat. The choppers and Honeywell grenade launchers onboard were finishing what Charlie had started.

It was all over in minutes. All that was left was a deafening silence and the light from a languid sun which filtered through the wispy patches of gunpowder smoke which drifted lazily over the canal.

The monitor which had been caught in the crossfire was dead in the water and settling stern first into the canal. It was riddled with bullet holes and RPG explosions. Two of the crew members were floating facedown in the mustard-colored water with crimson eddies seeping from their bodies. While one of the other boats maneuvered to fish out the bodies, we pulled alongside the destroyed monitor. What confronted us next was a scene right out of a slaughterhouse. The gutted insides were splattered with blood and brains and bone. The patrol officer's head had been blown off by a rocket. His body and another crewmember's looked like bloody pulp. They were just shapeless piles of bone, and tissue, and blood soaked nylon. Once again, the devastating power of modern weapons floored me. It was heavy duty.

Miraculously, one of the guys was still alive, screaming his head off in pain. We got to work scooping the gore into poncho liners with some helmets. Buddy and Bernie loaded the remains into our boat while I tied a tourniquet onto the near severed hand of the survivor. We headed a safe distance down the channel to a low lying area and called in a dust-off to evacuate the wounded man.

It wasn't until the chopper lifted off that the impact hit me. That's when the adrenaline withdrawal catches up, and the terror of a fire fight really overwhelms you. It really zaps you when you start to wind down and have time to think and reflect. I tried lighting a cigarette but my hands were shaking too badly. I grabbed a beer from the cooler and drained it into my parched mouth. I was drenched in sweat from the ordeal. Though I had reacted with seasoned proficiency, I was emotionally drained by the experience. No one onboard was saying anything as we headed back. I remember looking at the blood smeared deck and mangled remains and staring up into a low slung sun and feeling sick inside. Such a wholesale waste was still hard for me to stomach.

But what grieved us the most was the sight of Brothers standing on the pier with his Instamatic camera in total disregard of the tragedy.

13

Bloodlust

It didn't take long to be introduced to the beastial insanity of Vietnam. I'll never forget the sensation of throwing the boots of a friend into a chopper bay with the stumps below the knees still attached, or having the brains of the guy sitting next to you splattered all over your face from a high velocity round, or cradling a teenage buddy in your arms with his intestines spilling all over your lap as he cries in agony. I'll never forget the chilling sight of cracked and sunbleached jungle boots protruding from the cover of green poncho liners or the sickening sweet smell of rotting flesh, or the putrid taste of creamy yellow bile rising in your throat from the sight of fellow comrades lying like piles of bloody pulp on the deck of an incoming boat.

They were sights and sensations you never got used to. Oh, you sought to adjust. You learned to callous your feelings, half paralyzing your emotions, even denying reality. You did what you had to to protect the last fleeting vestiges of sanity. But short of a bullet to the head, there was no way to totally escape the horror. 'Nam was a ghastly kaleidoscope of tormented impressions which confronted you at every turn. You either numbed the pain with alcohol or learned to ventilate your anger in the most brutal of ways.

But what affected me the most was the V.C. atrocities toward the innocents. I hated the communists with a passion, but not all the Vietnamese. The ambiguities and butchery of Vietnam soured some guys against all orientals. To them, they were all gooks, dinks, slopes, zipperheads, slant eyes, but not to me. Some I came to love, especially the children.

I'll never forget the gruesome sight of pigs rooting among the remains of villagers who had been staked to the ground and disemboweled by Viet Cong in reprisal for supporting the South Vietnamese government. I will never forget the feeling of holding a six-week-old baby in my arms while he screamed to death. His body had been charred a reddish-black from a V.C. satchel charge which had been mindlessly tossed inside a Catholic orphanage. I just stood there looking at the overturned cribs and charred walls with fat tears running down my face. "How could something human do this?" It made no sense.

Then there was the coldblooded sight of a nine-year-old girl lying limp in the outstretched arms of a Korean Major whose men had found her on patrol after a squad of Viet Cong had raped and fileted her flesh with their bayonets. Major Kim commanded an R.O.K. detachment downriver. He was as tough as they came and had acquired a feared reputation in our area for extracting information from unwilling V.C. Prisoners. But even Major Kim was shaken by the brutal crumple of humanity. I tried to sustain her with a blood transfusion. We put her on our PBR and rushed her to a hospital upriver. But, I never knew if she made it or not.

Incidents such as these accelerated the hardening process, but one incident in particular finished the work.

The V.C. had a sadistic tactic which they manipulated to turn the villagers against the Americans. They would sneak a few men into a village and wait for a helicopter to fly by, then they would open up and didi mau back into the sanctuary of the jungle, leaving the innocent villagers at the mercy of gunships who thought they were taking hostile ground fire from a V.C. stronghold.

When they pulled this trick on a village downstream, a couple of Cobra gunships came in with the chainsaw rasping sound of their electric Gatling guns and chopped the brittle bamboo hooches to pieces. Most of the villagers had taken cover in their makeshift bombshelter tunnels adjoining their dwellings, but one teenage girl was stitched up the middle by the indiscriminate bursts as she darted for safety.

Some of the villagers brought her to us in a sampan to see if we could undo the damage. She was a mangled mess of pulverized flesh. She was lying in a pool of blood and dirty water which was gently sloshing in the bottom of the boat. She was barely conscious. Her thighs looked like someone had done a sloppy job of hacking large chunks of flesh from her bones. The 7.62mm rounds had torn out her female organs and layed open her abdomen, exposing her stomach and intestines. It only took one look to see she wasn't going to make it. I had enough medical experience to know that she only had a few hours to live. I knew that there were no adequate medical facilities in our area. She would die a slow, agonizing death.

It was one of those moments when you must make a painful decision which will live within your thoughts and dreams for a lifetime. I could keep her alive and prolong her agony for a few more hours until the excruciating pain and trauma took its inevitable toll. I could put a bullet into her pretty face and end her suffering. Or, I could give her three syrettes of morphine and let her slip into a deep sleep from which there's no return. She was already in shock and an overdose of morphine would O.D. her in minutes—quietly, painlessly.

Her distraught mother and father were hovering over us

jabbering in Vietnamese. They were just poor, illiterate rice farmers who thought I could save her with my little medical kit of dressings and scissors and injections. She just laid there in the bottom of the boat whimpering. I'd seen guys hit not as bad as she who were screaming their heads off and bawling like babies. I could speak a little Vietnamese, so I tried to comfort her; "You are a brave young lady." She couldn't have been more than 14. "What a lousy waste," I thought.

I asked her father what had happened. He responded tearfully in the clippity-clop sound of Vietnamese, using handing jestures to explain that a helicopter had shot up their village. When I heard that, I felt like crawling under a rock. I knew it was our guys. I knew it was a tragic accident, but that didn't make my predicament any easier.

The only compassionate thing I could do was to give her the three syrettes and tell her parents that they would help her go to sleep.

It was all so crazy. Here I was kneeling in bloody water in the bottom of a sampan from an innocent Vietnamese girl who I had just put to sleep out of a vague sense of mercy. Back home my friends were still cruising the strip on Friday nights, stocking supermarket shelves with Cheerios, or kicking back watching "Laugh In." Life for them had stopped in time, while I endured a grim slice of hell half a world away. When I got back, nothing would have changed. They would still be on the same merry-go-round. How could they understand what I was going through? How did you write home and explain; "Dear Mom and Dad, today I overdosed a 14-year-old girl because she was going to die anyway in 24 hours. Yesterday, I held the charred body of a baby in my arms and watched him scream to death. Tomorrow I'll throw the torso of a friend into a helicopter because it was all that was left of him after a firefight."

After a while you were so numbed by the butchery and so far removed from the world you left behind you just dried up. You stopped writing. How many times could you keep telling Mom comforting lies like, "Everything's just great, Mom. You ought to see the sunsets over here," when you were living in such a hellhole? I knew they couldn't handle the raw truth. They probably wouldn't have believed it anyway. Even though my letters home were few and far between, my parents wrote steadily, encouraging me to write more and send home money to save up for a car when I got back.

For the first few months, Michelle wrote two to three letters a week. They were the ultimate "care" package from home. But then they began to taper off to a slow trickle before they abruptly stopped. It was a pattern which repeated itself with heartless regularity in 'Nam. For some guys, the letters just stopped arriving. For others the oblique obituary arrived in the form of a "Dear John" letter. They came from fiancés and sweethearts and even wives who had promised their all, for better or worse, 'til death do us part, but they decided to exercise their option somewhat earlier.

Some were downright merciless. It wasn't enough to simply say it was over. They'd stick the knife in and twist it by enclosing Polaroid snapshots of themselves with new boyfriends in sexual acts while smiling and waving back like they were having the times of their lives. We had a bulletin board set aside in our compound for "Dear John" letters. It was plastered with letters and snapshots tacked to it—like statistics chalked on some battalion scoreboard.

At first, I figured she must be overwhelmed with school work. Then I thought a couple mail choppers got shot up. I kept writing Michelle but nothing came back. I finally wrote my parents and asked them if something was wrong. They only knew that she was in college and tried to reassure me that everything was probably okay. Silent weeks drifted into months. I finally wrote Michelle's parents out of desperation, asking if she was sick or something. They sent me a polite, if not formal reply, informing me that she hadn't been feeling well lately. What was that supposed to mean? Well, I wasn't stupid. The truth was like taking a hollowpoint in the stomach.

Much of our lives revolved around those letters from a sweetheart or wife. Sometimes, they were the only thing that kept you going. They were the last remaining link, the last fragile lifeline to the world. When that lifeline is cast off, we were left to drift deeper into the insanity which surrounded us. Except for your boat buddies, who too could be taken from you in a moment, you were alone.

Experiences such as these devastated you emotionally. Coupled with the carnage of 'Nam and the pointless harassment of our officers, they turned your heart to granite and fed an insatiable lust for revenge. They wounded you deeper than any piece of shrapnel and caused you to hate with such a bloodlust that you relished the thought of payback.

We were pulling a typical two boat night ambush along one of the jungle compacted sloughs off the Mekong. "Buddy" Mercer was up front in the twin .50 guntub. Ryan Bittner was amidships manning an M-60 and the radio. Bernie Fletcher was watching the towering treeline with the aft .50. I had grabbed a sawed-off Savage 12-gauge and headed a few meters into the jungle to check out our perimeter. I was dressed in my tiger greens with my face and hands smeared with camouflage grease sticks. It was that twilight time when the jungle grows still, when the lush greens begin to fade to grays, when shadows begin to create figments in the mind. Even the local coalition of mosquitos had temporarily withdrawn to regroup for the night assault. I popped some dexadrine and squatted Indian style in a cluster of multi-fingered fronds to watch and listen. I was all eyes and ears. My sensors darted purposely back and forth scanning the jungle through the unearthly half light of nightfall. Nothing was moving. It was a peaceful moment of refrain before the night creatures began their nocturnal search for food.

Several hours passed. The jungle's blackness had enveloped me in complete darkness. I could hear the subtle sounds of tiny creatures off in the brush and the occasional screech of a jungle bird high in the canopy. Just then, to my right, there was a rustling of leaves then something jumped onto my thigh, darted across my lap, and scampered off into the undergrowth. It happened so quickly, I barely had time to flinch. The surge of adrenaline so unnerved me that I was frozen in fear. My heart was pounding so hard, I could feel it in my throat. I was so rattled I don't think I could have fired my shotgun with any coherence. I went to my knees panting so furiously from the overdose of adrenaline that it was like I'd held my breath for several minutes and was desperately gasping for air. I had never realized rats got that big in 'Nam.

My system was still recovering from the rush when I heard the grumbling sound of the diesel engines. It was a signal for me to get back at once. I scurried back through the undergrowth and slid down the slimy bank to our boat. "What's up?" I asked Buddy. "We just got a call for help from Major Kim's compound. They're getting overrun." I half slipped along the bank until I found the bow line anchored to some exposed roots with a grappling hook. I unhooked it and climbed onto the bow as Ryan gunned the engines full throttle. We were flying down the dark canals navigating by the light of a starlit panoply.

Off in the distance, we could hear the confused chatter of automatic weapons. We shot up the Mekong, then turned up a side canal which dead-ended in a wide cul-de-sac at the R.O.K. compound. By the intensity of gun fire and light bursts, it seemed like all hell had broken loose. Each man took one last look at his arsenal. The weapons were locked and loaded. I could barely hear the metallic "clinking" sound of my sawed off M-14 as I pulled the bolt back and let it slam shut chambering a round. Ryan down throttled as we rushed into the cul-de-sac. Buddy cut loose with the twin .50's on figures rushing the barbed wire perimeter.

The battle was a scene of absolute pandemonium. The garish illumination of hissing parachute flares cast elongated shadows across the landscape. The silhouettes of frantic men were outlined against the background of grenade bursts and claymore explosions. Interlacing red and green tracers lasered at all angles.

The angry staccato of M-16's mingled with the methodic cracking of AK's and the distinctive "ta tow tow tow . . ." of M-60s. The blinking muzzle flashes from onrushing waves of V.C. heralded an all-out assault. A satchel charge had blown up some gasoline drums sending orange fireballs mushrooming into the blackness. The quivering flames bathed the water's surface with an eerie orange glow. The lifeless bodies of several V.C. sappers were outlined in the light, grotesquely snarled in the razor sharp concertina wire. Buddy, myself and Bernie were firing frenzied bursts like madmen at V.C. on the bank. Ryan maneuvered the boat toward a sampan approaching the shore. We were pulling closer, when I noticed several shadowy figures with AK's crouched in the shallow hull. As if by second nature, I stood up and without warning cut loose on full "Rock and Roll" screaming obscenities at the shadowy figures. I sprayed the sampan, chopping through the flimsy craft, splintering wood, bone and flesh, and kicking up geysers of water.

Two of the V.C. dove overboard and splashed frantically for the nearby bank. I ejected the empty magazine, rammed another one home, and cut them to pieces while I screamed at the top of my lungs, "Get some! Get some!" Ryan pulled the boat alongside the riddled sampan listing to one side as it slowly settled in the water. The bodies of three V.C. were sprawled in the boat. They weren't moving, but I was beside myself. Such was the all consuming rage and passion for revenge that I crammed another magazine into my M-14, chambered the round, then emptied them into the lifeless bodies. After the last casing flew free I paused, then turned to Buddy. I looked him in the eyes and with stone-cold sarcasm said, "I just wanted to make sure they were dead!"

The look on his face told me more than words. It was one of fear and shock; I had crossed the last frontier of morality. I had killed with cold blooded relish.

The back of the assault had been broken. The sporadic firing tapered off as the remaining V.C. melted back into the jungle, leaving me standing on the deck staring fiercely into the blackness.

14

Dust-Off

In May 1969, after re-upping for my second tour in 'Nam, the 524th Riverene Section was transferred to Tan An for "Operation Slingshot" (TF 116) and reassigned to the 573rd Riverene Section. We were stationed on a floating barge midriver in the Vam Co Tay. What was left of the original crew segregated themselves in their own cluster of bunks. All that was left of the original group of "Mekong Headhunters" working under the direct supervision of the CIA through SEAL Team One was Buddy Mercer and myself. Our tours had gone back to Na Bhe' in '66, My Tho'—'67, Sa Dec—'65, and now Tan An. But the group had been broken up one by one. After three years, Bernie completed the maximum number of tours and went home. Ryan had been court-martialed for hitting one of our officers in the face with a six-pack of beer. That only left Buddy and myself. Others had come and gone. Many would add their names to the polished black panels in Washington, D.C. years later.

Some fit in, some didn't. One particularly obnoxious individual was a religious freak we sarcastically called

"The Preacher Man." He bunked underneath me and incessantly strummed away on his old Stella guitar, singing preachy songs which irritated Buddy and I more than the persistent whine of Vietnamese mosquitoes. He in turn referred to us as "Pervert Number One" and "Pervert Number Two."

By the summer of '69, Buddy and I had drifted deeper into our reclusive world. As a consequence of losing too many friends, Buddy and I had drawn a tight circle around ourselves. Both of us had become almost obsessed with not forming any new relationships. It just hurt too much to read any more letters from sweethearts, or see any more family snapshots, or zip up any more body bags with your friends inside. I was sick of grieving parents writing me asking what their son's last day had been like. I had my fill of wives asking me how their husbands had died. We were both wearing emotional flak jackets to protect what was left of our feelings.

Countless missions had somehow merged into an overriding feeling of numbed tension and weary nerves. My last mission started little different than the rest—the same routine, the same worried uncertainty.

Sometime in July, we were out on a night ambush drifting with the current. I remember listening to Armed Forces Radio in Saigon and hearing Neil Armstrong saying, "One small step for man, one giant step for mankind." I'll never forget staring up into the sequin-sprinkled sky, watching a full luminous moon and thinking, "We've got the technology to land men on the moon but we can't end this crazy war." It was like I was living in the Twilight Zone.

There were no premonitions preceding my last patrol. The tension was there, but we'd pulled so many missions it had become routine—like deer season back in Michigan, except it lasted 365 days with no limit. It was in July. It was another night ambush in a free fire zone. We had license to shoot anything that moved.

We were beached along a muddy root-clotted bank with

intermittent jungle growth overhanging the river. We'd positioned ourselves around a bend in the waterway to intercept any Viet Cong sampans who might be attempting a night run. A new guy named Kenny was sitting on the bow keeping his ears tuned to any sounds in the jungle. It was about 3 A.M. in the morning with a scudding overcast interrupting the moon's glow. It had been raining off and on throughout the night. Droplets from passing cloudbursts pattered in a steady rhythm which occasionally rose in intensity as it thapped on the boat like impatient tapping fingers before subsiding to a muffled drizzle. The last shower had ended minutes before, leaving only the moist sound of dripping from the jungle growth. The air was cool and wet and fresh. Gossamers of mist floated in broken veils above the water.

Unbeknownst to us, another PBR was drifting silently around the bend on our blind side. It had picked up our rough outline against the bank with a Starlight scope. It was a two boat patrol of new guys from another section who were sneaking off of patrol early. They were green and inexperienced and trigger happy. They must have taken the wrong turn and inadvertently cut through our ambush area. No friendlies were supposed to be in our sector.

Buddy and I were sitting on the engine cover sipping an early morning beer when the lone crack of a rifle rang out, followed by the groan of Kenny sprawled backward over the bow with his legs dangling into the guntub. All we could think of was being overrun by V.C. in minutes. I told Buddy, "When I open up with the 60, get the boat off the bank and let's get the hell out of here."

I cut loose with the 60 sending scarlet slashes probing toward phantom targets somewhere in the jungle. Instantly, an angry hailstorm of machine gun fire behind us answered my report. Fluorescent streaks cut through the blackness, criss-crossing our boat with thousands of rounds of armor piercing tracers which found their mark as they plowed into the boat or ricocheted into the blackness like popping sparks.

Under the labored cough of the diesels, Buddy frantically struggled to back us off the shore. The river and bank erupted in geysers which splattered us with silt and mud and water. Someone on one of the PBR's was hand cranking their Honeywell grenade launcher. "Pop, pop, pop," the rounds bracketed the boat with blinding flash bulb explosions. "Get us out of here!" I yelled as I stuttered away with the 60. Just then, I was flung backward by a violent blast. My body felt like someone was whipping me with a hot wire cable. All I could think about was getting back to the M-60 before we got overrun. I pulled myself up and cut loose again when I was lifted by a grenade blast and hurled backwards. I was flaying the air when a burst of machine gun fire stitched me the length of my right leg from my calf to my groin. I slammed back first into the engine cover and slid to the deck. As I lay there, several more rounds punctured the fiberglass hull and tore into my body.

I could feel the boat shaking from the concussion of incoming grenades. Buddy was still trying to back the boat off, but she'd taken so many hits she had settled on the muddy river bottom. He was desperately gunning the diesels, but we were sucking mud. I was choking on diesel fumes and blood from chest wounds. My body felt like mush. I was soaked in diesel fouled water and warm blood. The shooting abruptly ceased. It had only taken a few minutes. I could hear the sound of voices screaming. My ears were ringing. Everything was black. Buddy was kneeling beside me crying and cursing at those who had done the shooting. He had figured out who it was. He gently cradled me in his arms and propped me against the engine cover. My fatigues were soaked with blood. Suddenly, I felt so very cold.

Buddy was beside himself. A torrent of emotions overwhelmed him as he cried and cursed. He was wiping his eyes with one hand and clutching my shoulder with the other. "Don't die, Mickey. Hang in there. We'll get you out." I was only vaguely aware of another PBR pulling alongside and the apologetic voices of other men. I mustered enough strength to ask, "How many dinks did we get?" But all Buddy could say was, "I'll get those . . ."

Diesel fuel and stagnant river water were sloshing around my legs. It felt like someone had poured gasoline into raw wounds. I remember the static hiss of a radio and someone screaming into the mike for a dust-off. I could hear the words, ". . . get it now or he isn't going to make it!"

It felt like my right leg was barely attached. Buddy and I had a long standing pact that if one of us got hit real bad, the other would end it for him. Neither of us wanted to go home blind, or crippled, or without our manhood. But he tried to assure me it was just a bunch of shrapnel wounds and I would be all right. I started to cough and retch up blood and bile. I was gagging and spitting up blood and trembling from the wet chill. Buddy scooped me into his arms. He was crying again. He was shaking me and muttering to himself, "If anyone's going to die, they are!" I didn't know that "they" were the green boat crews that had hit us.

I was fogging in and out, teetering on the brink of death. I could hear others crying and telling God how sorry they were. In the distance, I could hear the mournful sound of chopper blades slapping though the moist, pre-dawn air. There were hands lifting me up and lying me on a poncho liner. I was lowered over the side as men carried me up the slimy embankment, slipping and cursing. They carried us to a small clearing along the bank and laid us in the matted grass. I could hear the sickening sound of Kenny's chest wound wheezing and gurgling next to me. Buddy was kneeling beside me, demanding that I live. The resonant slap-thumping of rotor blades buffeted the rough LZ in the downdraft as the Huey hovered in. I heard someone ask, "Is he dead or is he dying?" Somebody said, "He ain't going to make it."

My eyes were burning and blinking from blood. Everything was a blur of shadowy images. I was floating into the darkness as they carried me to the chopper. I don't know whether I passed out or lapsed into shock, but I saw Jesus hanging on a cross with a thief nailed next to him. He was looking down at me with sad pleading eyes, and I remember feeling so very, very sorry.

15

Homeward Bound

My dust-off was about the last straw for Buddy. He was the only one left, and without the underpinnings of our friendship, he couldn't face much more time in the bush. He'd been fighting since '66 and was reaching the limits of his endurance.

Two weeks later, back at the river barge, Buddy stormed into the Company Commander's office and laid in on the line. "I quit! That's it! No more patrols, no more ambushes, no more seeing my friends wasted. Court-martial me, do what you want to, but I've had my fill of this stinking war. I resign, and if anyone tries to mess with me, I swear I'll blow up this barge and take as many with me as I can!" He wasn't asking, he was telling him the way it was going to be, or else.

Whether the C.O. understood or feared the consequences of getting fragged, I'll never know. For the next sixty days, Buddy Mercer strapped on his .45 automatic and sat in solitude in a French cafe in Tan An, drinking "Tiger Beer," silently watching the war pass him by.

The war was passing me by in other ways. I barely made

it to the 3rd Evac Hospital in Saigon after I got hit. I was only half conscious of the desperate attempts to keep me alive.

The E.R. was a bloody scene of orchestrated chaos. Last Rites had been given to a dying Protestant, but I was still clinging to life. The traumatic wounds and massive loss of blood had brought me precariously close to death. My thoughts were reeling through a murky fogbank of confusion. I was weak and only vaguely aware of activity around me.

Someone had cocked my head back while a nurse was trying to push some plastic tubing down my throat and insert it through my airway. I realized it was a plastic trach tube. They must have known from the coughing, gasping sounds that I was having difficulty getting air, so they were trying to open up the restriction. But the plastic tubing was cutting off my oxygen even more. I started to retch and gag. A surge of adrenaline-inspired energy flowed from a will to live. I reached up with my good hand and ripped the trach tubing out of my mouth, then leaned on my right elbow and screamed, "You mother . . . are you trying to kill me?"

Just then, I felt someone touching a pressure point on the side of my neck. There was a sharp sting then everything went black. The next few hours were a semiconscious nightmare. It was a bizarre purgatorial half-state of tortured impressions—a hellish limbo between life and death. I'd come out of my drug induced haze, completely terrified, screaming my bloody head off, and see doctors suturing my leg or probing my chest cavity with forceps. There were dulled sensations of tugging and cutting. I'd drift away, then I'd come to and see field surgeons in splattered green smocks hovering over me. They were removing bullets and serrated slivers of shrapnel from my leg and arm and dropping pieces into an emesis basin.

I remember blurred fishbowl-like impressions of bright lights and I.V.'s of plasma, and bloodcurdling screams from someone else in the room. At one point, it seemed like someone was reaching down a deep dark tunnel and was pulling me upward toward the light. At another, excruciating pains snapped me back to reality. It felt like my leg had been removed and someone had clamped a pair of channel lock pliers onto my exposed femur, and was trying to wrench the bone right out of the socket. I was screaming and crying, "Oh God, it hurts, it hurts. Stop the pain, please!" Then I would feel the prick of a needle. A nurse was injecting more morphine, then I'd drift off again into a dreamy state of detached numbness.

So began my painful descent into the grim netherworld of a field hospital's Intensive Care Unit. After yards of silk sutures and gauze and surgical tubing, I was deposited on the Dirty Orthopedics Ward in I.C.U. It would be the first in many agonizing stopovers on my long journey home.

The ward had the gruesome appearance of a human slaughterhouse. It reeked with the disgusting, half-death stench of burned flesh and blood and body fluids. It was filled with young men who had been delivered from the bush with traumatic amputations of arms and legs. Some beds cradled only the pathetic remains of a head and a torso. Life support machines and tubes ran all over their mangled remains pumping up and down and in and out, trying to keep them alive. The screaming on the ward never seemed to cease. Stripping away unwilling layers of blood clotted gauze, debriding raw wounds, or inserting stainless steel pins through shattered knees and joints elicited a ghoulish chorus of pain from men who could endure no more.

For critical days, I lingered near death in I.C.U. lapsing in and out of consciousness, never escaping the agonizing pain. At times, I could feel the gentle touch from a nurse or a sympathetic smile before my eyes grew heavy and I'd pass out. After several days, my condition started to stabilize. I regained consciousness and my first feelings of hope that I would make it.

That's when the Viet Cong sapper squads hit the air field in the pre-dawn darkness. I remember flinching in pain at the first sounds of the attack. The hollow coughing sound of mortars electrified my system with surges of adrenaline. I looked around the ward and saw the telltale look of terror on the shadowy faces of crippled men. It was the claustrophobic look of bedridden men in the straightjacket of an intensive care ward—men bound to cables and tubes and pins and traction and I.V.'s and life support systems. Men without legs to run or arms to grasp. You could feel the nerve-fraying suspense as men waited for the inevitable. "Karumph!" The first mortar exploded somewhere across the field. "Karumph, karumph, karumph!" The V.C. mortar crews were cratering the tarmac and aircraft revetments in erratic patterns. The Quonset hut shuddered from the concussions, jiggling the I.V. bottles with a glassy tinkling sound.

"Karumph!" The explosion was closer. Men were squirming in their beds and looking around in wide-eyed terror. Somebody was demanding, "Hey, what's going on? Get us out of here!" "Karumph, karumph!" The maniacal bursts were walking toward us with terrifying regularity. The concussions slammed into the corrugated siding. "Aaaah! Get me out of here! Get me out of here!" someone was screaming. There was a deafening explosion, followed by the wailing sound of shrapnel as it tore into the walls like a knife through a beer can. "Karumph!" There was a blinding orange flash and a gaping hole was torn through the ceiling at the end of the ward. The sounds of crashing glass, screaming men, and toppled bed frames filled the ward. I.V. bottles of saline and blood were flung from their supports shattering in a crystal shower of sharp glass and crimson splinters.

Several medics threw themselves over immobilized patients and were peppered by a blizzard of shrapnel. "Karumph!" The acrid smell of burnt cordite mingled with the nauseating smell of blood and vomit floated through the half gutted ward. A nurse who had been hiding behind the nurse's station dashed across the open ward in response to screaming men. "Karumph!" A second round disemboweled the ward. The blast caught her in mid-stride, lifting and twisting her upward like a rag doll before dropping her to a crumpled heap on the floor by my bed. She was lying motionless staring across the floor with a glassy, fish-eyed look. The back of her dress was torn and soaked with a huge red splotch.

The ward was a scene of pandemonium. Hysterical, panic-stricken patients screamed in terror or fought for survival. Men were ripping I.V.'s from their arms or trying to crawl out of the ward. Others were trapped and unable to move. The sense of helplessness was psychologically overwhelming. We were strapped in the electric chair waiting for the switch to be thrown. Men who thought they'd gotten out of the jungle alive were facing death once again without any way out. All we could do was scream and pray for the dawn.

I spent several weeks at the 3rd Evac Hospital in Saigon tethered to three I.V.'s, a pin in my mangled right leg, and my left arm in a cast. My body looked like raw hamburger. When the doctors felt I was stable enough to move, they took me by ambulance to a C-141 Starlifter parked on the apron at Tan Son Nhut. It was a Medevac flight for critically wounded men heading for specialized wards in military hospitals clustered around Tokyo.

Our C-141 served as an enormous air-ambulance. Scores of young men were carried into the cavernous bowels of the plane and secured to tiers of stainless-steel bunks lining the fuselage. There seemed to be almost as many nurses and corpsmen as patients. It was the beginning of a painful passage to Japan and eventually home. We were a battered collection of torn nerves and tattered flesh. Some were horribly burned, with 3rd-degree burns from ruptured gas tanks or phosphorous grenades. Some were bandaged so completely that they only had slits for eyes and airways. Many were amputees from booby traps. I remember the jostling of stretchers and jiggling I.V.'s giving the impression of a wind chime as they carried us onboard. We were all in a glassy-eyed daze from doses of Demerol and morphine to dull the pain. Still, even the slightest movement tortured our bodies.

In moments, we taxied into position and screamed down the runway in our final farewell to Vietnam. Several hours later, we touched down in Yokohama, Japan. We were loaded onto ambulance buses for an agonizing trek through the crowded, potholed streets to an Army hospital. The bus driver seemed like a sadistic maniac. He slammed on his brakes in endless stops and starts in his attempts to avoid cars that cut in front of us. He lurched forward in excruciating lunges, honking the horn and grinding gears as he wove his way through the endless traffic jams. The flight had wearied weakened bodies to the point where every jar amplified the pain. I'll never forget the stagnant heat in the un-airconditioned bus and the grimy smell of thick smog which choked the crowded streets.

When our convoy of buses reached the hospital, a number of us were placed on gurneys and wheeled up to the 5th floor where we were placed on the "Dirty Orthopedics Ward." Everyone on the ward had some form of serious staph infection—some due to arms and legs being blown off, others because napalm or phosphorous burns over large portions of their bodies, and still others whose flesh had been terribly shredded by bullets or explosions.

It was another halt in my gradual transit home. I spent six agonizing weeks in intensive care in Japan: weeks of debriding dead tissue, cleaning away infection, of endless injections, of surgery and skin grafts, and traction, and probing damaged nerves, and draining sores, and incoherent screams. It was a time of electrifying pain and oppressive monotony, when time dragged by in slow motion and days washed into dismal grays.

I had been hit nineteen times by machine-gun bullets

and shrapnel, taking the brunt of the injuries the length of my right side. It was a miracle that my right leg was even attached. Huge chunks of flesh had been blown away from the impact of .50 caliber slugs and my femur had been shattered in two places. It was due to the severity of my compound fractures and mutilated leg that I was placed in dirty orthopedics. The top of my left hand had been blown off to the bone by a grenade blast. What was left of it was held together by wire cable called "K-wires" to prevent atrophy. They intended to keep my bones properly spaced until they felt I was stable enough to graft the backside of my hand to my stomach. When I got back to the states, they planned to make an incision across my stomach, peel back a thick flap of skin, and sew it to my hand. It would remain attached to my stomach with ace wraps while my flesh grew to my hand.

I would spend six weeks in a precarious balance between life and death.

I seemed to have floated through an incoherent dreamscape for several weeks, sedated and numbed against the ever-present pain. I'd made it this far; the dust-off, emergency room, Last Rites, mortar attack and Medevac flight to Japan were behind me, but I was still in critical condition. I was a pathetic remnant of my former self, battered, broken and bloodied. Any one of a dozen possible complications could place me in an aluminum casket bound homeward for burial at any moment.

The complication that came was purely by accident. The surgeons had inserted a stainless steel pin through my right leg and had grafted the femural artery off of my left leg back to my right in a desperate attempt to salvage what was left of my right leg. The procedure required that I lay absolutely still in bed.

One of the orderlies was making his routine morning rounds adjusting the patients by cranking up their beds. Someone had fouled up and failed to inform him that my bed was not to be disturbed. When he started cranking me into a sitting position, I felt a ripping pain followed by a hot liquid feeling under my thigh. I reached down with my right hand underneath my right thigh. When I pulled my hand up, it was drenched in fresh blood. I called to the medic who was cranking three beds down. I held up my blood-covered hand and said somewhat quizzically, "Hey, Doc, look at this!"

There was instant panic on his face. He could see what I couldn't. He could see an expanding pool of blood from a crimson fountain that was gushing from the severed femural artery. His face was ashen colored. It was a study of emotions, but the shock in his eyes needed no explanation. He scrambled toward me half falling over himself in haste screaming for the doctors. His panic panicked me. "Whoa, what's goin' on!" I thought. He grabbed a snakelike piece of amber rubber tubing, threw the blood-splattered sheet off of me, and tied a tight tourniquet just above the hole in my right femoral artery where all my blood was spurting out. A swarm of doctors and nurses descended upon me like starving vultures on a carcass. I was losing precious pints of blood which had to be replenished immediately or I would die. It was absolute chaos. Doctors and nurses were slipping and sliding in the slimy pool of blood trying to figure out what to do.

One of the emergency room doctors arrived and inquired, "What's his blood type?" "O Negative" was the reply. "We've got to get blood in him fast!" An orderly ran for pouches of whole blood and returned in seconds. A stopwatch atmosphere prevailed as they rushed to beat the clock. They were having difficulty registering an I.V. needle. My veins had collapsed from the massive loss of blood. I had had so many I.V. injections since Saigon that my arms looked like a veteran junkie.

There was no time to waste gently trying to find a vein or artery. I needed blood now or I would be dead in seconds. The doctor was cursing in frustration when he yelled out the ominous words, "Cut down!" I knew from my medical training what the dreaded "Cut down!" meant. They would have to go beneath the surface to find an artery.

There's a large artery in the center of your arm. A cut down is peformed in the inside hollow where your arm bends at the elbow. They take a scalpel and insert the blade about an inch and a half into the hollow and slice backwards about three inches. Then they probe with their fingers inside the incision until they locate the artery.

They had no time to numb my arm or wheel me down to the O.R. They couldn't risk giving me any pain killers because I was going into shock and if you give morphine to someone in shock they may never come out of it. They just O.D. I was half insane with fear. I remember reaching up with my left hand and grabbing a black corpsman by the throat and pulled his face down to mine, looking him in the eyes and saying, "Boy, don't you dare let me die." His eyes got saucer shaped and he lost the color in his face. He wrenched free and grabbed my shoulders. Three other corpsmen helped him hold me down. Two of them held my shoulders and arms while two held down my legs.

The doctor took a glistening scalpel from a tray. Without any ether or zylocaine or sodium pentothal he jammed the scalpel into my arm like he was skewering a rump roast and sliced back in one stroke. Then he layed back the flesh until he found what he was looking for and inserted a gigantic gauge I.V. needle into the artery. I was forced to lay there for several hours while they pumped blood into me before they wheeled me into surgery.

I had crossed any reasonable thresholds of pain. I was screaming my head off, begging them to put me out of my misery. They were tearful screams of utter agony pleading, "I can't take it, please kill me. I'm not going to make it. O.D. me! Give me morphine and O.D. me. For God sake kill me." I'd black out and come to screaming, then I'd black out from the pain. I'd regain consciousness because the pain was so excruciating and I'd wake up again screaming my lungs out. The nightmare kept up for hours until my blood pressure leveled off to a safe area. Then I was taken into the operating room for arterial grafts to hopefully repair the damage.

My close call with the ruptured artery was about all the trauma my right leg could withstand. The multiple wounds, shattered bones, and borderline circulation created the perfect conditions for infection to set in. On the week of my 22nd birthday, some of the nurses brought me a cake and we had a little bedside party. A couple days later I was wheeled into O.R. and my right leg was surgically removed just above the knee. I was informed later that my heart had arrested on the operating table and the doctors almost didn't get me back. I was then transferred to the amputee ward next to dirty orthopedics.

I remember laying on the ward with scores of guys who had lost part of their manhood, feeling sorry for myself. It was about ten at night. A couple of officers had been making the rounds with boxes of medals they were handing out to men or pinning to their pillows. I had three glass intravenous bottles pumping plasma, whole blood, and antibiotics into my body. A chorus of bottles along the length of the ward began to tinkle against each other as they hung suspended from stainless steel poles. Then my bed began to slide. I didn't know if I was dreaming or hallucinating or what. Just then, a nurse yelled, "Earthquake!" I couldn't believe what was happening. I'd gotten shot by my own men, mortared in the hospital, nearly bled to death, had my right leg amputated for a birthday present, almost died on the table, and here I am on the 5th floor in the middle of an earthquake.

I was psychologically raped at that point. I looked and felt like a piece of carved meat. I was sharing a ward with a bunch of guys who could never walk again, never caress their wives, never hold their children. I no longer felt like a man but a freak that belonged in a sideshow. I was going home to a society that worshipped youthful virility and beauty, and here I was without a leg to stand on and a hand that looked like it had been crammed into a meat grinder. I was suffering from a deep "castration complex." All I could think about was suicide. "How could I get one of the nurses to give me enough pain killer to O.D. myself?"

The final insult to injury came when a musician came to our ward to entertain the patients. We'd get pretty actresses or beauty queens through every so often passing out glossy 8″ x 10″ photographs with their autographs. Sometimes we'd get entertainers. They were brought in to cheer up the guys and boost morale. But this guitar player backfired. He strolled down the aisle singing folk ballads. He paused in front of my bed and started singing, "Where have all the flowers gone." It was bad enough feeling like half a man—a legless, near armless freak fit to be discarded on the dungheap of humanity and I've got to listen to, "where have all the soldiers gone, gone to graveyards everyone, when will they ever learn, when will they ever learn. . . ?" He probably meant well but it seemed like the cruelest of jokes.

After six weeks, the doctors scheduled my Medevac flight home. It was a bittersweet moment when I said goodbye to the doctors and nurses who had fought to pull me through. I was wheeled on a gurney to a chopper pad emblazoned with a large circular red cross. A medical Huey was waiting to fly me to a small hospital at the Air Force base I would be flying out of. They'd numbed me up pretty good for my departure, but I was still conscious of what was going on. I was lifted off of the gurney by several orderlies and lowered onto a stretcher. They were carrying me to the bug-shaped chopper when the pilot ignited the engine and the rotors began their methodical wind up. I remember the co-pilot looking out of the plexiglass cockpit with his sun-visored helmet and turning back to his controls. I was placed onboard and strapped in by a medic.

The blades were slapping toward lift-off when the crew chief gave a thumbs up to the pilot. That's when it hit me. I was having a flashback. The chopper tilted forward then climbed and beat its way over the smog blanketed city. I started to scream, "They're going to shoot us down, they're going to shoot us down!" I was freaked out. The medic was trying to calm me down, but I wasn't in Japan any longer; I was back in Vietnam. It wasn't until we landed and I was safely off-loaded that I regained my composure.

I was scheduled to spend two days on a small ward while I waited for my flight home. I had reached a point of depression from which there seemed no return. That night an orderly brought me a tray of food and laid it on my chest. I had very little movement. My left arm was a mixture of plastered gauze and stainless steel K-wires and my entire midsection was covered in a spica body cast.

I took one look at my meal and decided I didn't have the patience to hassle eating it with one hand. I was struggling to reach for a pack of Pall Malls lying beside me on the nightstand when I caught a distinguished looking Air Force nurse out of the corner of my eye putting on her coat. She was leaving for the evening meal. She walked past my bed, then turned around and came up to my side. "Soldier, you need a smoke?" she must have observed me struggling. "Yes Ma'am. It's a little hard with these casts." She reached down, pulled out a cigarette, and placed it in my mouth. Then she picked up my Zippo when she noticed an inscription engraved on it, "For those who have fought for it, freedom is a taste the protected will never know." I could tell by the expression on her face that the saying hit home. She looked up at me and said, "I know you can smoke a cigarette, but how are you going to cut your dinner up with just one good hand?" It was blunt, but not insensitive. "I've come this far, I'll manage somehow." But my voice betrayed the self-doubts

and defeat that was slowly gnawing away at my insides.
"I'm not in that much of a hurry." She slipped out of her
coat and sat beside me cutting up my food and feeding
me. She spent the next hour with me on her own time. It
was a timely touch of compassion which I so very much
needed at that moment.

16

No Pain, No Gain!

The time had come for the last leg of my journey home. A host of ambulances converged on the air base to unload their wounded into the waiting bowels of another C-141 Medevac flight back to the world. I was bolted into a Striker frame to minimize my movement. By chance, I was the last patient carried onboard. They positioned me along the fuselage wall next to the door. I remember hoping that the door was properly secured. I didn't want it to blow open at 38,000 feet over the North Pacific. If the cabin was suddenly depressurized, I would be the first one sucked out, and with my luck thus far I had come to expect the worst.

We lifted off through a dreary morning haze into toneless gray skies. It was a monotonous flight which arched over the North Pacific. We touched down in Anchorage in the summer twilight of an Alaskan night for refueling. We were all heading to hospitals back home, but that knowledge did little to relieve the pain which punctuated our passage. Bandages still needed to be changed, I.V.'s checked, and pain injections administered to men who had lived with constant, sometimes unbearable, torment for weeks.

We lifted off once again and touched down in the morning at Scott Air Force Base, in St. Louis, where we were scheduled to spend the night until we were transferred to our respective hospitals in the morning. When we taxied to a stop, the wearied staff of nurses and medics made final preparations to offload us. The door was opened and several stateside medical attendants came onboard. Since I had been the last one on, I would be the first one off.

I'll never forget this one wise-guy nurse who started to demonstrate how to double check the Striker frames. My Striker frame was assembled in such a way that my body was bolted in from both sides so that I could be rotated at intervals to lessen the risk of developing bed sores. I was secured in my stainless steel rotisserie by bolts at my head and feet. The male nurse had forgotten to re-thread my foot bolts in his inept demonstration. They started to rotate my frame when the contraption collapsed, sending me crashing into the floor, stump first. The plunge ripped out I.V.'s and sent bottles shattering to the floor. I was screaming in pain and cursing for a gun to shoot the idiot. One of the nurses grabbed a Demerol syringe and mainlined it into my arm through one of the I.V. needles which was still taped to my arm. I was in never-never land in seconds. It was a rough welcome to the states.

In the morning, I was placed on a small air ambulance and flown to Glenn View Naval Air Station on the north side of Chicago. A special ambulance was waiting there to transport me to Great Lakes Naval Hospital.

It would be my third trip to Great Lakes. Once again, I was assigned to a dirty orthopedics ward—Ward 3 South. They were wheeling me onto the ward past the nurses station when I asked the head nurse how long before I could go home. My question elicited a round of hearty laughter. "Son, you won't be going home for quite a while." I didn't need to hear that. I was in a morose mood, feeling pretty sorry for myself. It was as if a resident black cloud followed me onto the ward. The sobering sight of those same 80 beds and 160 flags hit me with the force of a baseball bat. Nothing much had changed except the occupants. I was no longer a naive orderly tending to the wounded. I was one of them.

I would spend a year and a half at Great Lakes before I was released to outpatient status.

The philosophy of the medical staff which prevailed on the ward was one of optimism, tempered with a frank dose of realism. I remember grimacing in pain and clutching the side rail with my right hand as a doctor stripped away caked dressings when he took note of my ordeal, and with a wry smile, looked me in the eyes and said, "Hey, no pain, no gain." It was a short, but fitting commentary on the realities of Ward 3 South.

Still, I fought a relentless battle with depression. The depressing sight of disfigured men, coupled with the repugnant medicinal smells of antiseptic solutions and sour body fluids served as a constant reminder of my fate. The reactions of visitors often did little to relieve the despair. Some came willingly during visiting hours, others came out of a grim sense of duty. They were fathers and mothers, wives and sweethearts, brothers and sisters, friends and acquaintances who were trying to cope with the carnage in their own awkward ways. But there's no easy way to face the grotesque sight of raw draining stumps, blood stained gauze, 3rd-degree burns. Mostly adolescent men lined the bulkheads with horrendous wounds. Not only were limbs conspicuously missing, but some had horrible head wounds—missing jaws, noses, parts of their skulls. Some were so grotesquely deformed you could barely look at them without turning away in reluctant disgust.

I was so lonely—so desperate. Outside of the support of fellow patients and the medical staff, the only thing that kept some of the men going was the weekly visit of a loved one. My parents and a few friends came to visit me, but what I wanted most was Michelle. I wasn't much to look at. Months of intravenous feeding, nausea, and the amputation of my right leg had reduced my body to an emaciated 85 pounds. I had been a robust 188 pounds before I was hit, but I now looked like one of the living dead in those grainy black and white newsreels of Nazi Death Camps.

Maybe in some subconscious way I wanted her to help reaffirm my manhood and restore a purpose to live. But I had received no word from her for months. No "Get Well" cards or letters of support had caught up with me in Saigon or Japan or Great Lakes—not even a postcard saying, "I heard you were wounded." I got a lot of cards from friends and acquaintances who knew my parents, but nothing from the one person I needed to hear from the most. It was as if she had dropped off the planet Earth.

When my parents came to see me, I asked them where Michelle was. I could discern an uneasiness in their eyes and an evasiveness in their response. There was something stilted in their voices. What could they say. It was awkward enough just seeing me in my condition, let alone being put on the spot concerning Michelle. My dad knew what she was doing, but they couldn't bring themselves to tell me. She had dropped out of college, moved in with some girls, and was doing a lot of partying.

I had pressured her to break off our engagement before I left, secretly fearing she would take me up on my offer. I had tested her emotionally and failed. She had stood her ground and promised she would love me no matter what. She would be there when I returned and nothing Vietnam or anyone else could do would quench the love she felt for me. On this, I had pinned my hopes. It was this reason for living which I carried through all the nightmares of 'Nam.

Two months passed before Michelle mustered enough courage to come up to visit me. She came with her parents—probably out of constraint. She only came because her parents had forced her. They must have felt she owed me at least a final visit. She called and said she was coming and told me she missed me. But I couldn't help detecting a nervous strain in her voice. I wanted things between us to turn out all right. I was desperately grasping inside for something to cling to. I had to have a reason for living. I needed her to say, "I love you, Mickey. Everything is going to be okay. I'm here now. Just hang in there, we'll make it together. You'll see, it's going to be the way it was before."

I felt more nervous awaiting her visit than going into combat. So many fragile hopes hung on the outcome. What would she say? How would she react when she saw me lying in my emaciated state looking like a cancer patient in the terminal stages?

I knew only too well what could happen. We tried not to look, but we couldn't avoid the pain of a fellow patient when a wife or fiancée came to their bedside and said, "Hey, I am sorry, but I can't be married to a cripple. I'm still young and have needs. I just can't take this." They would turn around and walk away, leaving some poor guy hanging there. He wasn't going anywhere with no legs and three I.V.'s stuck in his body. The I.V.'s and radios would still be playing, but you could feel the oppressive silence which settled in the aftermath of such encounters.

When Michelle came up to see me, I was blown out by her beauty. She was as lovely as ever, but she'd taken on a more seasoned sensuousness since I'd seen her last. Her blond hair had grown to her shoulders and she was wearing a tight mini-skirt which reached halfway up her thighs. But I could tell the sight of me lying there with the sheets depressed around my right leg, I.V.'s hooked to my body, and my left hand wired with K-wires had completely unnerved her.

I remember her sitting on the side of my bed stumbling through some meaningless small talk like "How have you been?" Michelle had never smoked when I knew her, but she reached for one of my Pall Malls, took a deep drag and exhaled out her nose without so much as a blink. All I could say was, "Wow, you sure have been busy." She looked away for a moment then looked back and smiled. "Well, what are we going to do?" I said.

Why prolong the pain, I thought? We might as well get it over with one way or the other. She said, "Hey, everything's fine. Everything's going to be okay." But her response was somewhat wooden, like she had rehearsed it, like she was mechanically reciting what I wanted to hear. "Listen, Michelle, are you sure you don't want out of this deal? I guess you can see I'm not the same person I was before I left." "It's okay, Mickey. I told you I would be here when you got back, and I meant it. I've already found an apartment in Chicago and will only be 45 minutes away. I'll be able to drive up and see you as much as I can. It will take time but we can put this relationship back together and try to pick up where we left off. You'll see, everything is going to work out." She bent over and gave me a passionate kiss which elicited a chorus of cat calls and whistles, then smiled and left the ward.

That was the last I saw of her. A day went by, then a week, then three weeks. I was hoping against hope, but deep down in my gut I knew it was over. I called her house a month later and asked for Michelle. Her parents were shocked. They thought she had already told me the day she came to the hospital. They didn't want to hurt me, but they told me what Michelle could not bring herself to say.

She had told me exactly what I needed to hear. She just didn't have the heart to let me down hard. She'd been with other men who hadn't left her for 'Nam. We had both changed. Things could never be the same again. We were victims of two different worlds which neither really understood. We were both casualties of Vietnam—wounded in our own ways an ocean apart. Looking back, I don't know how I would have reacted if the tables had been turned and Michelle had been horribly maimed in an automobile accident. What if she had been disfigured or burned and I had come back from 'Nam without a scratch? Would I have stayed with her?

The realization that she wasn't coming back caused the bottom to fall out. My romantic house of cards came crashing down around me. There seemed nothing left to live for. The doctors had already told me it might take ten to fifteen years and over thirty operations to repair the damage. It was all too much for me to take. Rejection can be so devastating, but to be rejected when you're disabled only compounds the hurt.

Other guys' wives and girlfriends were coming to visit them, but my visits were few and far between. Grand Rapids was a long drive from Illinois. I couldn't really blame them. It was hard to outsiders to stomach the sights and sounds and smells of the ward. The medicinal smells of a dirty orthopedics ward could unsettle the strongest stomach. The unnerving sight of mummified stumps, gauze wrapped burns, and stainless steel pins through joints was too much for most to take. The sounds of an eighteen-year-old Marine clutching the guardrails of his bed and screaming in pain from scab-caked dressings being removed was too unbearable for some parents to endure. Every visit was an emotional ordeal for my parents. They tried to show support in their own awkward ways. They told me to be tough and try not to feel sorry for myself, but what I needed most was someone to hold me, cry with me, absorb my hurt, feel my pain. But they could barely cope with their own.

The first year I spent Christmas alone on the ward. Everyone else had been discharged or sent home for the holidays. I had three TV's and five Christmas trees surrounding my bed. I spent my time in solitary confinement watching ballgames and parades at the same time on a half-lit ward with seventy-nine empty beds wrapped in clean white sheets. I just layed there hooked to I.V.'s and stoned on pain killers only half oblivious to the loneliness.

Groups came through the wards from churches, Boy Scouts, and the Red Cross singing carols and passing out goodies, but I was the only one on the ward. They'd all tell me how sorry they felt for me, but I would shrug it off like "no big deal." Yet inside, I was slowly dying.

I couldn't flick on the TV without Hollywood reminders of how things should have been. This one Pepsi commercial tortured me with its romantic images of a bronzed hunk strolling hand in hand along a deserted beach with a gorgeous bikini clad girl. It hurt so deeply to realize that I would never walk down a beach with some beautiful woman in tow. I couldn't imagine myself ever wearing a bathing suit, let along hobbling through the sand with a mechanical leg. I couldn't stand that commercial. I'd change the channel or turn off the set, anything not to face the reminders.

Crushing despair followed in the wake of her departure. As far as I was concerned, Great Lakes was not a stopover in my painful pilgrimage back to the world, it was the end of the line. I couldn't bear the thought of a bleak future of deformities, countless operations, prosthetics, V.A. hospitals, pain, and loneliness.

There were those around me who confronted their fate with determined dignity and unassuming courage. A few withdrew into a sullen shell or lashed out with anger and bitter cynicism. My self-pity had turned to anger then to abject hopelessness. I had reached a point where I felt I had nothing left to live for. I hated life and did my best to make everyone around me pretty miserable, especially my parents.

My dejection was only compounded by the news reports we viewed each night on the television sets along the walls. Every week, the body counts followed us home. And there were the scenes of anti-war demonstrators protesting by the tens of thousands in the Capitol Mall, the Pentagon, college campuses, and even outside the gates of Great Lakes. But the galling images of long haired protesters burning draft cards and torching the American flag while waving the North Vietnamese flag in defiance tore us to pieces. "This is what we had been fighting for? This is what we sacrificed our bodies for?" we asked ourselves.

When the My Lai incident hit the wire services, it seemed the news media bent over backward to castigate Lt. Calley and every other Vietnam Vet who ever served. It only fueled the chronic contempt toward the stereotypical nineteen-year-old soldier who did nothing in 'Nam but rape, pillage and murder innocent Vietnamese. But you took one look around the ward at the mutilated men and you wondered what war they were talking about.

It was more than we could comprehend. Not only had America turned her back on the war, but she had turned her back on her sons who had gone in good faith. It was painful enough facing a fraction of your former self, but the galling sense of national rejection and self-righteous contempt was a pain we couldn't bear.

Our Dads had come home to ticker-tape parades and banner headlines. But for us, there were no "Welcome Back" banners when we returned. There were no brass bands, no festive parades, no cheering crowds, no fireworks, no flag waving. We found little pride or patriotism—only protests and profanity.

It was especially galling for those broken men who lined the ward—those quiet heros who laid their lives on the line out of the patriotic conviction they were doing what was right and honorable, only to discover they had fought a thankless war for an ungrateful nation.

For the first few months at Great Lakes, the doctors were not even certain I would make it, and they were justly concerned. My left hand was so mangled, they nearly amputated it. If it had not been for my caring father's vehement protests, they probably would have. Five months were spent with my stump mending and my left hand jury-rigged with K-wires before I was operated on to graft my hand to my stomach. My heart arrested a second time during the operation. My lungs had been so weakened from anesthesia, I had to spend three weeks recovering under an oxygen mask.

I was a pretty pathetic sight with a leg missing, my left hand sewed to a stomach flap, and an assortment of tubes running in and out of my body. I'll never forget the shock on the faces of two voluptuous Playboy Bunnies who had been sent to the hospital from the Chicago Playboy Club to pass out complimentary copies of that month's issue and cheer up the boys. They weren't expecting the shock when they came bouncing up to my bedside. It was like they had run into a brick wall. The stunned reflection on their faces was a depressing reminder of just how pathetic my condition really was.

But inevitably, the pain and rejection forced those of us on the wards to pull together, to draw some measure of solace from each other's support. It wasn't the by-product of some mutually shared martyr complex or because misery loves company, but the result of men who were unalterably affected by a common experience. John Wayne, Motherhood, and apple pie may no longer have seemed real, but the near sacred camaraderie we "forgotten few" shared was. It was one of the redeeming elements of 'Nam that managed to survive, even on Ward 3 South. At times, it seemed that my sanity depended upon their support. Their constant care, often under the duress of their own private hell, drove me back from the brink on several occasions.

So devastating was the initial despair that I was close to a complete psychological breakdown. I had reached a point where my coping capacity was shot. Just how close I was at first to going out of my mind was driven home when an old high school friend came to visit me. Peter Denning was in the regular army stationed south of Great Lakes at Fort Sheridan. He was trying to cheer me up with updates on old friends when his voice and the sounds of radios and TV's on the ward began to fade out. I could see his lips moving, but I could barely hear him. It was like I was 50 feet underwater. I said, "Can you hear me talking?" I could see by the quizzical look on his face that he was confused. "I'm losing it, I think I'm going out of my mind. I'm afraid I'm going insane, Peter. Just keep talking to me, I'm going over the edge." The panic in my voice sent fear flushing over Peter's face. He started to get up as if he was going for help when I pleaded, "Please don't leave, Peter, cuz if you do, I'll never make it back!" His eyes bugged out in wide-eyed terror. But he just kept talking until the sights and sounds colored in around me.

17

Henry

I'd reached rock bottom when a couple of very special patients took me under their arms, not out of pity but empathy. We may have suffered in our own private worlds, but there was a corporate suffering which we all identified with and shared. When some guy was crying out in pain a few beds down, he was crying for all of us.

Cary Cassella was a Marine from Oak Lawn, Illinois, whose legs had been severely wounded when another grunt on their patrol tripped a captured claymore. They stuck him in a bed next to me on the Plastic Surgery Ward. Seven hundred ball bearings had ripped through half a dozen men, turning a couple guys to mush and stripping huge chunks of flesh from Cary's thighs and calves. It was a miracle he had any legs at all.

When they sewed my hand to my stomach, I thought I looked weird until I saw Cary with both of his legs crossed and grafted together.

Cary had a very vivacious girlfriend named Cindy, who he later married. She was a real sweetheart who took it upon herself to sister half the ward. Cary's indomitable courage and her unflagging support did a lot to maintain some semblance of sanity as I weathered my long night of the soul. I'd been on pain killers and intravenous feedings for so long I had very little appetite. Cindy was always teasing and pestering me to eat with the persistence of an Italian mother. The pain was so annoying, I had little desire for food, but Cary and Cindy would pressure me to eat a few bites. Sometimes Cary would jump in my face and threaten me to eat or else.

His family would come up to visit. They adopted me with the affection shown to a stray puppy their boy had brought home. They went out of their way to encourage me. Anything I wanted, they'd get. I remember having a craving for a juicy orange. The next visit, they brought me a huge basket full of several dozen. They picked up Cary's crusade to restore my appetite by bringing us special foods we didn't get in the hospital. There weren't too many Baskin Robbins, pizza parlors or McDonald's Golden Arches in the Mekong or Great Lakes, so they made up for it. Thanks to their support, I managed to tip the scales at just over one hundred pounds by late winter 1970.

But another guy named Henry touched me in a much more profound way. Henry had been a Marine grunt. A white phosphorous grenade had blown up in his hand. Phosphorus is a hellish chemical. At a safe distance, they explode with an almost deceptive beauty. They blossom into graceful umbrellas which shower molten streamers of white hot phosphorus which burns with an insatiable heat. It burns through everything, even under water. When it hits your skin it clings like fly paper and literally eats its way through your flesh until it burns out. The only way to stop it from burning is to cut off its supply of oxygen with mud packs.

Henry had been in a firefight, had popped the spoon off of a phosphorous grenade and had just cocked his right arm back to throw it when an AK round slammed into his chest knocking him to the ground. He landed on his back still clutching the willie-peter round when it burst, blowing off his right hand and showering his body with a rain of liquid hell.

I'd seen a lot of random phosphorous and napalm burns, but nothing as gruesome as Henry's. For most, it took an almost morbid curiosity just to look at him. He looked like a piece of plastic that had melted. His scalp, eyebrows, and eyelashes had been burnt off leaving only scarred slits for his eyes. His ears had melted off and his nose was reduced to a grotesque nub with flared nostrils. His body was covered with ugly marbled scars and his fingers on his left hand had burned away to tiny stubs. The flesh on his chest and stomach and genitals had simply melted away.

And yet, he carried himself with a noble dignity. Henry was a humble, soft spoken sort of guy. He had an unassuming air about him which had a calming effect on those around him. We all felt somewhat humbled in his presence.

One day, I was feeling sorry for myself—sorry because Michelle had left me, sorry because they'd taken off my leg, sorry because half my hand was missing, sorry because I was in constant pain—and Henry shuffled up to my bed. I didn't see him coming, but when I caught movement out of the corner of my eye, I looked up and saw this horribly scarred young man standing beside me in a faded blue hospital robe. He didn't say anything. He reached out his left hand with his stubby fingers and dropped a package on my lap. It had fallen upside down so I couldn't tell what it was at first. I reached down and turned it over. It was a small picture frame with a portrait of one of the most handsome, blond, blue-eyed Marines in dress blues I had ever seen. Then it hit me. It was Henry before he had been mutilated by that grenade. All he said was, "That used to be me." It was spoken not out of self-pity but as a blunt point of fact which he was trying to accept. It was as if he was saying, "Hey, listen

Buster, before you crawl into some hole and die, it could have been a lot worse. You could be me!"

That sobering little encounter blew my mind. I mean I felt lower than a piece of paper on a wet street. I was still reeling from the first words when he added in a wistful voice, "You know, I had a wife and two little kids, but when I got to the hospital back in the states, my wife walked into the burn ward and saw how viciously scarred I was. I mean, I didn't even look like a human being any longer, just some grotesque freak. She walked up to my bed and didn't say a word. She just squirmed out of her wedding and engagement rings and laid them at the foot of my bed. With a cold, calculating voice she looked down at me and said, 'I can't live with this. I've made up my mind that I'm not going to be married to a cripple for the rest of my life. You're an embarrassment to me and the kids.' She turned around and walked off the ward. I haven't seen her or my kids since."

They tried to get you to go home on weekends as soon as possible. It was supposed to be therapeutic. They wanted to create a bridge back to society, but it wasn't that easy. Even Henry's parents didn't want him home. In their own roundabout way they'd let him know that it was too hard on them seeing him the way he was. I don't know what happened to Henry. I asked my plastic surgeon one time if he knew what had happened to Henry, and he said he didn't know. Maybe they dumped him in some V.A. hospital so he wouldn't be an embarrassment to society any more.

Our ward endured the fullest spectrum of pain, from mild aches to raw excruciating torment. We weathered every conceivable description—sharp, piercing, pinching, stabbing, gnawing, throbbing, burning, tearing pain—emotional, vexing, worrying, agonizing, remorseless, teeth-gritting pain—pain that respected no persons, gave no quarter, reluctantly yielded to relief. We knew them all.

The perpetual pain and depression drove many on the ward to retreat to the numbing consciousness of alcohol. Some of us became consummate boozers and veteran drug addicts. I consumed oceans of beer in Vietnam but steered clear of drugs. We knew how to handle our limits with alcohol, but getting stoned had all the built-in uncertainties one would expect from a straight juicer. I think we each feared freaking out in a firefight because we were too stoned to control our thoughts.

It wasn't until I was wheeled onto Ward 9 South for plastic surgery recovery that I first inhaled the pungent, sweet smoke of marijuana. My first hits off a joint observed all the well-worn rituals—hand rolled ZigZag joint pinched between thumb and forefinger, a deep drag sucked in between pursed lips, a couple choked back grunts, and a victorious exhale. I didn't feel anything at first, but before I realized it, I was "Oh wowing" with the best of them.

Some of the soldiers and Marines had really gotten turned on to grass over in 'Nam. You could buy baggies or sandbags full of the choicest Cambodian Black and prerolled cigarette packs of the stuff laced with potent opium. Some of the guys were more legitimate stoners by the time they came back than a California hippy. A few of the ambulatory patients on the ward served as gophers to purchase booze or score dope for us when they left the ward. These guys would return from a shopping spree with grocery bags brimming with fifths of whiskey, gin, scotch—you name it. Every time they came back it was like an alcoholic Santa was making his rounds.

The constant suffering helped justify our self-induced attempts to kill the pain. You can get pretty desperate when every waking moment is spent in physical torment. We would drink ourselves into oblivion or smoke joints until we couldn't see straight—anything to relieve the pain. There was little for us to do except watch TV, listen to the radio, and try to escape the hurt by numbing our nerves and our minds.

The doctors would make their rounds every morning between 7:00 and 7:30 A.M. to check the charts and re-schedule medications. Some mornings the ward smelled like a brewery. Wastebaskets and nightstands were spilling over with bottles and beer cans. But we didn't care. What were they going to do, bust a bunch of amputees and stick us in the brig or discharge us with dishonorable conduct after sacrificing arms, legs and looks? But the doctors never said anything. They acted like they didn't see a thing. I guess they realized it was the only recreational release most of us had.

There was an unspoken sympathy from the doctors and nurses. They knew we weren't faking the pain. They didn't want us to suffer, so they were religiously punctual in ad-ministering pain killers at the specified times on our charts. I became a scrupulous clock watcher, like a rat at feeding time. My eyes never strayed long from the hands of the clock. We were junkies waiting for the next fix—not so much to get off or expand our minds, but to dull the edge. We lived for those shots with the same obsession of a confirmed alcoholic who lives for the next drink.

Sometimes, our commitment to each other caused us to trade shots. If the guy laying next to you was hurting too bad, and we could hold on for another hour, we would give them our shot. The corpsmen were tremendous. They bent the rules to help a fellow Marine or suffering soldier any way they could.

I spent nearly seven more months on the Plastic Surgery Ward enduring my stomach graft and plastic surgery to restore my left hand. Most of the time, I stayed higher than a kite stoned on alcohol and drugs. Nearly a year and a half of drug therapy had turned me into a legal addict. That status would follow me for the next thirteen turbulent years.

During the last few months of my hospitalization, they

changed my status to ambulatory in their goal to gradually wean me from the hospital. I was allowed to go home on weekends, but they were little more than drunken binges with other out-patients.

On one weekend outing, I was riding back with a couple of Marines who lived about thirty miles away from my folks. We were weaving down the interstate in drunken abandon when we lost control and skidded off the freeway into a shallow culvert. My face went through the windshield, slicing it up pretty good. I had cuts and scrapes all over my face and was covered with blood.

When the uniformed state troopers arrived, they took one look at me with blood splattered all over my shirt and lap from my facial lacerations, saw my leg missing, and thought I'd lost it in the accident. When I came to and saw the flashing red lights, blood, and ambulance attendants, I totally freaked.

Once again, I was in 'Nam fighting for my life. The state troopers and attendants were trying to talk me down, but I was back in that blood smeared chopper bay with my life draining out of me. My parents rushed to the hospital when they were notified of the accident, but when they arrived they were shocked to find me crazed with paranoia. I was like a wounded animal whose paw has been caught in a trap. I was backed into a corner in my mind, and lashing out with violent outbursts at any attempts they were making to console me.

I don't think they believed I was having a genuine flashback. Maybe they thought I was putting them on or grandstanding for attention, but they couldn't comprehend the depth of reality I was experiencing. I'd been back in the states for over a year, but I had lived with reminders of the trauma of Vietnam jungles every day.

The ward did little to deprogram us. It was like trying to reform a convict in the midst of a prison full of hardened criminals. The constant suffering summoned us all back to 'Nam. You couldn't just turn the momentum off like a light switch. It was easy taking the soldier out of the war, but it was another matter taking the war out of the soldier. Returning to the states was the easy part, adjusting to the monotonous mainstream was a psychological absurdity. I'd flourished in a pressure vacuum too long to acclimate to normalcy overnight. I'd spent a year and a half in 'Nam coiled tighter than a steel spring and unwinding wouldn't come easy.

I had lived a hair's breadth from death on an adrenaline rush for so long, coming cold turkey off of my run would be fraught with intense withdrawals. My physical senses had grown so acute that they couldn't adjust overnight to the normal sights and sounds we take for granted back home. Even the shelter of Great Lakes did little to defuse the conditioning. The backfire of a passing car, a casual tap on the shoulder, the sound of a helicopter's blades slapping overhead, a simple walk across a lawn, or being suddenly awakened from sleep triggered instant responses conditioned by the sustained stresses of combat.

The Special Forces could teach you how to waste people with proficiency, but they couldn't teach you how to return home the same way you left, especially when you were physically and emotionally mutilated by the experience. Back in 'Nam, there were times when I thought I had grown numb to the suffering and death. Sometimes I felt as though my conscience had been castrated, but I was finding out just how vulnerable I was in the traumatic aftermath. I was a walking war zone—an emotional basket case—burdened with conflicting emotions fluctuating between bitterness and fear, depression and rage—yes, especially rage. Each day, I struggled with reminders of my past and taunting reminders of the present.

18

The Zoo

After a year and a half, I was medically retired from the Navy with a 100% disability rating. What awaited me was a revolving door of V.A. hospitals, years of delayed stress and over thirty more operations to repair my damaged body. I was shuttled off to the V.A. Hospital in Ann Arbor, Michigan, located next to the University of Michigan Medical Center. It had such a despicable reputation for its filth and medieval care, we sarcastically referred to it as "the zoo." It was little more than a garbage dump for discarded veterans. Many of the wards reeked with the sour ammonia smell of old urine and dirty bedpans, and had the appearance of a derelict rest home. Decrepit old veterans from World War I and II lined the rundown wards. They were in all manner of disfigurement and paralysis. Many were wasting away from acute alcoholism, tuberculosis and emphysema. At night, you could hear their labored gurgling coughs as they wheezed and hacked thick globs of mucous from congested lungs. Occasionally, one of them would be coughing hysterically when you'd hear them let out a final gasp and die. The staff would let these "old-timers" lay there all night until the doctors made their rounds in the morning.

The place had none of the compassion of Great Lakes. You practically had to beg for a pain shot, but they acted like they were being rationed. The whole atmosphere was degrading. I felt more like a scrap of meat in a butcher shop than a human being. Even the doctors and nurses treated us with the same bored indifference of a worker in some tractor plant in Russia. Most of them were long-haired types doing intern work from the University Medical Center. They reminded us of the same crowds of protesters who marched in front of the gates at Great Lakes, praising Uncle Ho and spitting on the American flag. They treated us with cold indifference. We detested them with bitter suspicion.

I was fitted for my first prosthesis at the zoo. Comfort and fit seemed of minor concern. They just wanted to rig you with a synthetic substitute and be done with it. It wasn't quite as bad as "one size fits all," but it was close.

Orderlies pushed us down in wheelchairs and deposited us by the dozens in this long corridor outside the Physical Rehabilitation Department to await our fitting. We cynically referred to the clinic as the "butcher shop." There would literally be hundreds lining both sides of the hallway. You would sit there for mind numbing hours surveying the stainless steel wheelchairs and their crippled occupants, or staring blankly at the dreary green walls.

I will never forget the pathetic sight of one triple amputee slumped in a chair across from me. My heart went out to him. He was about my age with a frail young wife and two kids waiting with him, and the kids kept whispering, "Mommy, what are we going to do? What are we going to do?" There lives, like so many others along the corridors, were little more than a pile of fractured pieces— "Humpty Dumpty" lives which looked as if they could never be put back together again.

The wait was worse than an inner city welfare office.

Many of the guys were stoned on pain killers, drugged out in a glassy eyed stupor. After hours of waiting, my name was called prefunctorily with a dispassionate tone in the orderlies' voices. It was so impersonal, so demeaning. It was never "Mr. Block," just "Block." My name simply underscored the impersonal atmosphere. There were no smiles or courtesies, just stone-faced stares. All we were to them was a serial number and so many artificial limbs. We were nothing to them but animals who had managed to survive some grisly experiment.

They took a cursory glance at my chart and removed a plastic leg from a shelf with the same routineness of a shoe clerk at Kinney's. They were running an assembly line with a "hurry up let's get this thing over" attitude. An attendant demonstrated how to strap on the leg to my thigh, then had me walk up three steps and down three steps between two parallel bars. So much for my therapy. I was wheeled back to my room and within two hours, I was unceremoniously discharged from the hospital.

They never taught me how to walk, or how to carry my weight. They weren't worried whether it fit. The fit was so bad it rubbed my stump raw. My stump was so ulcerated it leaked blood from the crude fit. Over the following months, I'd come home and go in the bathroom and literally pour blood out of the socket. My treatment at the hands of the V.A. did little to soothe the bitterness and rage that was seething in my heart.

When I got out of "the zoo," I moved into an apartment with a Marine I'd struck up a relationship with back at Great Lakes. We both enrolled in school to take advantage of the vocational rehabilitation benefits entitled us under the G.I. Bill. But we were just going through the motions to reap as much money from the system as we could. We figured they owed us. So we stayed drunk or stoned most of the time and took just enough classes to get by.

Oddly enough, in spite of all the trauma I had been

through, I lived in constant suspense, half-longing for some lethal rush to interrupt the uneventful drudgery I faced each day. The constant pain and partying provided little purpose for my existence. Back in 'Nam, I had developed an obscene obsession with danger and excitement, and I found myself craving anything to get the juices flowing, even entertaining a repetitive desire to return to the jungles of 'Nam.

But interwoven with my secret craving was a passion to vent my hostility. I was so consumed with bitterness, anger and paranoia, I wanted to take it out on someone or something to relieve the pressure. I slept with a .38 Special tucked under my pillow and a .30 caliber carbine with a sliding stock and a 30 round banana clip stashed under my bed. I'd lay there at night with the door unlocked, just hoping some thief would walk through it so I could blow him away. I was living with a secret "death wish" to end the physical and emotional torment which wracked my mind and body every day.

On the bottom line, I'd gone past a life of quiet desperation. I didn't care whether I lived or died. I was eaten up with the cancer of despair. There was no motivation to do anything but to go to bars at night or smoke joints and crash out during the day. As far as I was concerned, there was nothing left to live for.

Nearly two years had passed since I'd gotten hit that July night back in 'Nam. The war was still grinding on and I was still paying interest on my wounds. The doctors had removed a miniature scrapyard of shrapnel from my body, but pieces were still working their way to the surface. When one large chunk created a painful bump on my left arm, I knew it was time to have it cut out, but there was no way I was going to readmit myself to "the zoo," so I asked my mother if she knew a good surgeon. She recommended one she knew in Grand Rapids.

When I called to make an appointment, a receptionist answered the phone with a sweet sounding voice. I had become so self-centered with a "world owes it to me" attitude, I lived entirely for myself. I grabbed the foremost and left the Devil the hindquarters. So I just brazenly asked her, "Hey, when are you going to take me out for lunch?" She just played along with my bold come-on like it was an innocent game.

When I arrived at the doctor's office, I met Shirley. When I checked in at the counter, she gave me a playful smile and told me to be seated. She had recently graduated from college with a degree in psychology and was working as a receptionist until she decided whether she wanted to go on to graduate school. She was a real sweetheart, but super naive.

After the doctor removed the piece of shrapnel under local anesthesia and bandaged up my arm, I left. When I got back to my apartment, I called her back up and asked her out for a date. She was attracted to my crude brashness, much like Michelle had been in her innocence. It wasn't long before we started dating quite a bit. She had a real heart of gold and a sympathetic ear which I was drawn to.

When I introduced her to my parents, the first thing they confided was, "she's too good for you." They even took her aside and warned her not to get too serious with me. They were being bluntly candid when they told her in no uncertain terms that I was an animal: "He'll hurt you. He'll let you down. You can count on it."

But in spite of their fair warnings, she hung in there. We were married in August 1971, almost two years to the week when my leg had been amputated in Japan. On the surface, it looked like my life was finally going somewhere, but the changes were only superficial. I had a beautiful wife whom I loved, yet inside I was harboring the same festering pocket of emotional pus. In spite of all the understanding and tenderness Shirley showed me, a storm was still raging deep within, and no amount of compassion or listening ear could calm the tempest.

We purchased a cute little Dutch Colonial house with a V.A. loan. Shirley worked full time while I went through low-grade jobs like toilet paper. I worked for a parts department in a Chevy dealership and a construction company and a half a dozen other mediocre jobs. I just couldn't hold one. I couldn't stand some meathead civilian bossing me around. Back in 'Nam I was a professional. I was entrusted with expensive equipment and called upon to perform tasks that would be impossible for someone back in the states. But I couldn't handle some yokel telling me off for grabbing the wrong item off a shelf or treating me like some gimp moron.

At every turn, the hurt was magnified. Sometimes I'd apply for a job and be turned down because of discrimination. The country was so fed up with 'Nam they didn't want some Quasimodo cripple dragging his bad leg around the store, reminding them of the tragedy. I took federal exams and passed with high scores, but I'd have employers look at my applications and DD-214 and stare me right in the face and say, "I'm not going to hire a Vietnam Vet—especially a disabled one!"

It didn't take long to fulfill my parents' prophecy. In short order, I proceeded to make Shirley's life miserable. I refused to allow her to dead bolt the door at night. I was half-praying that some slob would be crazy enough to break in so I could blow him away. I'd stay up some nights pacing the floor or sitting in a darkened living room with a loaded gun, drinking beer and waiting for the intruder who never came. Many nights, I never came home from work. I'd head for a bar and leave her home with the dinner growing cold and the table set for her new husband. Sometimes I would be gone all weekend.

For all intents and purposes, my life revolved around drugs and alcohol. The perpetual pain had made me chemically dependent. I had undergone one operation after another. I had developed a degenerative bone disease called "Osteomyelitis" and suffered from reoccurring abscesses

197

and infections. Hardly a day passed without pain pills. I ate them like candy. The only way I knew to escape the pain was to stay high or drunk. I'd walk into a bar and order six to eight drinks at one time. When I was doing a stint in Junior College to collect my check, I'd finish a morning class and head for the closest bar where I would have a liquid lunch and drink six drinks at a time until the bars closed at 2:30 the next morning.

She was such a dedicated wife. She strove to make things perfect, but I rewarded her by treating her like dirt. I turned her life into a living hell. Once again, I was hurting the one person who loved me the most. And what was truly a tragedy was the fact that she thought it was all her fault—like she had failed as a lover and a wife.

Not only was my life a wreck, but I managed to make our marriage a shambles. In my private frustration, I was bent upon making her life as unhappy as mine. I was merciless in my caustic cruelty. I tormented her constantly with verbal abuse, putting her down and crushing her self-worth as a woman. She was like a delicate flower which I ground under my heel. I was so demanding, I treated her more like a slave than a helpmate. I'd belittle and berate, rag away at every shortcoming. The house was never clean enough; the food was never good enough; she was never skinny enough; she never wore the right clothes; I couldn't stand her hair style.

She had stuck with me and tried to be a bulwark of strength even though I dragged her through a nightmarish odyssey of mental and emotional torture. But my waywardness finally wore her down. I guess she reached the conclusion that as long as I was going to hang out at the bars, she might as well go along. She concluded it was the only way to salvage what was left of our marriage.

But the party world I exposed her to only corrupted the marriage further. Any semblance of stability Shirley brought into our union was quickly undermined. Life in the fast lane exposed both of us to constant compromises which started to shipwreck our marriage. I'd been out of control for years and provoked Shirley to follow suit. Her love shriveled up and was gradually replaced by hatred. We had grown so far apart we could no longer stand each other. We'd managed to gut it out in our running civil war for over ten years, but both of us were empty and miserable. We finally decided to file for divorce. All we had to show for our endurance was a broken home and two shell shocked kids who had been emotionally devastated by our constant skirmishes and spitefulness toward one another.

Even after years of torment, I scarcely understood the depths of my wounding. I had come back so physically disabled and psychologically warped, I still hadn't recovered. All the pent-up anger and hurt from my past had followed me home. They could give me skin grafts, issue me a plastic leg, and pump me full of drugs, but nothing eased the pain. All the partying and boozing and unyielding resentment did nothing to relieve the psychological hell in my heart. I was so emotionally dislocated, a cure seemed nowhere in sight. Not only did I carry the painful baggage of my youth, but I had brought a garbage load of traumas back from 'Nam. Much of my condition was a result of my inability to put Vietnam behind me. I had all the classic symptoms of post-traumatic stress in the extreme.

I sought healing in the V.A. counseling centers for Vietnam Vets. They tried their best, but I found their treatment about as helpful as sticking a bandaid over a bullet wound. They could diagnose the presence of delayed stress, and even categorize it, but they couldn't heal it. All the rapping and reminiscing did little to unravel the tangled web of hate and despair. Often our sessions were little more than clinical counterparts to the sloppy drinking bouts I had with other stressed out Vets sharing sentimental bar talk.

Often, we left the rap groups worse off than when we came. We carried all of our simmering hate and bitterness into those meetings and left at a rolling boil. One by one, we'd pour out our grievances and end up stoking the flames of discontent even further. We'd get so wound up that at one point we concocted a plan to capture a nuclear power plant to make a statement. We all had access to personal arsenals of automatic weapons. Enough of us were hard core combat Vets and Special Forces types with such an attitude of reckless abandon that we knew we could pull it off.

Our relief was so shallow. All our rapping and combat reminiscings seemed to accomplish were superficial healings. The root problems were just too deep and too complex. It was only a matter of time before we returned to quietly drinking our lives away in darkened bars and small family kitchens.

After thirteen years, I finally reached a point where I just gave up. It seemed everything I had touched had spoiled. My life was shot, my marriage crumbling, my children shattered. I couldn't endure another day of hurt. I could no longer face the drugs, the bar crowd, the infighting, our children crying, the plastic leg. I could dull the pain with drugs and booze. I could climb into a pair of jeans to cover my leg. But underneath, I was still the same wretched mess.

So I decided to end it. A voice in the back of my head kept urging me, "Do it, go ahead. You're not a man any more. Kill yourself. It's over anyway. What do you have to look forward to?" Shirley had left and taken Jodi and Bryan with her. I didn't know when she was coming back, if ever. I went to the gun cabinet and removed my .357 Magnum, checked the cylinder to make sure it was loaded, then walked into our bedroom. The house was empty and quiet. I slumped on the end of our bed and looked at the gun in my hand. I'd wasted more men than I could count in 'Nam. It shouldn't be that hard to waste one more, I thought. I raised the gun and stuck the barrel in my mouth.

I started to apply pressure with my thumb, when I had a vision.

It was as if I was floating above the bed, looking down into the bedroom after the lone shot had rent the stillness. I saw my body sprawled on the floor at the foot of the bed. The carpet was stained with a large pool of blood. The wall was splattered with brains and blood from the magnum round. Then I heard the sounds of my little daughter Jodi, running down the hallway with my young son Bryan. I wanted to say something, but I was invisible. They skipped into the bedroom laughing only to run head first into the gory sight of their father with half his head blown off and the wall splattered with brains. I wanted to scream, "Don't look, don't look." But the damage was done. They burst into tears and screamed, "Daddy, Daddy!"

That's when I realized that pulling the trigger would not put an end to the suffering. It would destroy not only my life but the most beautiful gift I had known, my wife and kids. I withdrew the gun from my mouth and sunk to my knees beside the bed. Hot tears were flowing down my cheeks—the bottled up tears of a lifetime. I was not alone. I was kneeling before God with an empty soul and a body wracked by pain. In my supreme moment of despair, I instinctively knew where to turn. I had finally come to the end of myself. It was no longer a broken body which needed care, but a broken heart and soul. "God, I don't even know if you're real. But if Jesus really did die for me, I need you to take away the hurt because I can't handle it any longer. Please God, if you are real, please help me. Oh God, please forgive me for all that I've done against you and my family. I want you to come into my life and heal my mind and emotions. If you can take away all the hurt and bitterness and anger I've carried all these years. . . . I need you now. Not next week, not tonight, but right now!" I so desperately needed Him to take the weight of the ages off of my shoulders—the weight I had borne since I was a tiny baby in that crib.

There were no fireworks or angelic choirs, but there was a warm sense of knowing—an unspoken awareness that he understood the pain I was suffering and had heard my cry.

That afternoon when I accepted God's terms for unconditional surrender, I felt a profound peace sweep over my soul. It was as if a brooding stormscape had been rolled back by an unseen hand revealing the light of the sun. I pulled myself up from the tear-soaked carpet transformed by God's grace and delivered from oppressive years of guilt and anger and frustration. There was a strange feeling of wholeness I had never known before. My leg had not grown back, my scars were still unhealed, my marriage still shattered, but now I had an almost uncanny sense of peace which passed all understanding—like everything was going to be okay.

In view of my track record, my wife's reaction was understandably suspicious. She viewed my conversion skeptically, like I was pulling some scam to keep our marriage out of divorce court. She had every right to distrust my intentions. After years of unfulfilled dreams and broken promises, she wanted nothing to do with me or God. She wasn't buying into my new outlook on life and assurances I had changed.

But several weeks later and closer to divorce court, two of Shirley's cousins, who were our age, had suddenly died. The news shook her to the very core of her being and caused her to confront eternity with a fresh sobriety. Shirley surrendered her life to the Lord as well and agreed to try to put our lives back together.

It took time to heal the accumulated years of hurt which had destroyed our marriage, but God helped rekindle the love and restore our relationship with one another and our children.

Both of us had had a religious upbringing, but we

wanted more than the dead formalism we had known. We needed more spiritual reality than what we had grown up with in the "religious" institutions of our youth. We continued to visit churches for over a year, slowly growing in our newfound faith, but still unable to find a fellowship where we felt we belonged.

19

Pervert Number One

On Friday, July 2, 1982, Shirley was in the kitchen preparing lunch. She decided to turn on the radio and was playing with the dial when she tuned into a local talkshow called "Born Twice." The host said that his guest was a visiting evangelist and a disabled Vet who had been severely wounded in Vietnam. She called to me outside and asked if I would be interested in listening to an interview with a Vietnam Vet.

During the previous year, I had made my long pilgrimage home and had come to terms with most of my experiences in 'Nam. Still, it had been such a pivotal part of my life, I would never be able to completely put it behind me. I had been doing a lot of soul searching at that time, replaying certain episodes from that dark page from my past, reflecting on how the course of events had woven their way to this point in time. The Vietnam War was still very much on my mind. I suppose I knew that some things still needed to be resolved.

Several weeks before, I had received a surprise call from Buddy Mercer. He was scheduled to fly through our state on a business trip at the end of the week. He called and said, "Hey Mickey, can I come by and see you and Shirley?" "Sure, Buddy, we'd love to see you again." Then without really thinking, I blurted out, "You'll never guess what happened to me, I got born again!" For several strained moments there was dead silence on the other end. I didn't know if we'd gotten cut off or Buddy had hung up. "Hello, hello, do we have a bad connection? You still there, Buddy?" "Yeah, I'm still here," he said in a measured voice. I could tell he was somewhat taken back by my announcement. We talked a little more. He gave me his flight number and the time he would be arriving in Grand Rapids.

Buddy had loosened back up by the time he landed—the same old Buddy. It was a warm weekend of fellowship, reminiscing about the "good old days" and those moments that were not so good. We spent a lot of time comparing notes, trying to figure out what happened to the men we had known. Shirley had gone to bed and Buddy and I were in the kitchen drinking coffee late into the morning when Buddy confessed, "You know, Mic, what really tears me up?" "What's that, Buddy?" "Well, now that you're . . . well you know, born again, it seems real ironic." "What do you mean?" I asked, somewhat confused by what he was driving at. "You remember that guy named Dave Roever that bunked under you at Tan An the last couple of months before we got hit. You know—that Jesus freak we called the Preacher Man?"

Before Buddy could continue I cut him off. "Yeah, how could I forget. Remember how that guy got on our nerves singing all those religious songs on that old guitar and telling us all the time how much God loved us? At the time I couldn't handle that guy. My coping mechanism depended on whoring, boozing and killing. I just wasn't ready for all that God talk. At that point I had so climbed into my protective shell I just couldn't handle any new relationships. Well, you know what we were like. I especially couldn't handle that guy telling us about God. I guess that sounds kinda funny coming from me now?'' Buddy offered no response. ''The more he talked, the more defensive I got. I remember telling him at one point that he could take all his religion and shove it. I feel kinda lousy now when I think of all the times I tried to sabotage his walk by leaving *Playboy* magazines and beer on his bunk. But, you know Buddy, he never said a word. Man, I couldn't comprehend how somebody like him made it through all the qualifications of Special Forces training, let alone end up with a bunch of sickos like us. He seemed more like a youth director for some church camp than a navy commando. Remember when we'd sit on our top bunks facing each other with our legs dangling over the sides working our way through a case of beer and the Preacher Man would be strumming on his guitar beneath us? We would sit in the dark smoking cigarettes, popping tops and sucking suds, and we could hear him whispering prayers in the darkness, and I'd tell him to knock it off.''

''Yeah,'' Buddy smiled almost affectionately. ''Remember, Buddy, when he'd chuckle and shake his head and call me Pervert Number One and you Pervert Number Two? You know, I honestly didn't think a guy like that would last a week in the armpit. But he really proved himself. I've never seen anyone else trim a fifty like the Preacher Man. I've often regretted not being able to say goodbye to him on more friendly terms before I got hit.''

Buddy cut in, ''That's what I was trying to tell you, Mic. He didn't make it.'' ''Oh no, what happened?'' Buddy cleared his throat then continued; ''About two weeks after you got dusted-off we were out on patrol and his outfit got ambushed. I got there only fifteen minutes after the distress call. I'll never get over what I saw. It hit me harder than what we saw when that monitor got ambushed in the 'Devil's Hole.' It was horrible. He was just about to throw a phosphorous grenade when a round hit it. It blew up in his hand next to his head. Mickey, I'm not kiddin' you, man. He looked like a burnt marshmallow. That phosphorus had cremated half of his body. He was so burnt, the flesh was hanging off him in red-black tatters. His hair and ears and clothes had burned off and globs of phosphorus had burnt deep holes into his chest. When I found him, he was lying there smoking and charred, looking like a crispy critter. I mean it was so bad some of the guys were heaving their guts out at the sight of him. He was still alive when we carried him to the chopper, but there's not a snowball's chance in hell that he made it. I'll never forget his eyes looking at me from that poncho liner. They were almost pleading. The only person I felt more sorry for was the poor slob at Graves Registration who had to stick that charcoaled carcass in a body bag and zip it up.

"After that, something snapped. I just couldn't take it anymore. I only had 63 days left in my tour, so I went to the C.O. and told him I quit. I could see wretches like us getting wasted. We half deserved it. But it seemed like such a shame for a nice guy like Dave to get wasted. You know, Mickey, he was the only guy that ever told me there was someone up there who loved us."

Buddy's news of Dave was still haunting my thoughts that day when Shirley called out about the radio interview. If it had been any other talk show, I wouldn't have wasted my time. But I could relate to other Vets. We had both kissed death on the lips and survived. The host had already introduced his guest by the time I got to the kitchen so I didn't catch his name. Shirley placed my lunch in front of me while I listened to the show. The guest was responding to the interviewer's questions in a raspy voice. His responses were laced with familiar terms which instantly conjured up memories from the past. He talked about SEAL Team One, the 573rd, PBR's and being horribly burned by a phosphorous grenade.

I couldn't believe what I was hearing. Could it be the

Preacher Man? Then I thought . . . No! Buddy had told me himself that he was dead. He didn't have a chance in a million of making it. He'd thrown his charred body onto the chopper—thirteen years ago in the Delta. But who else could it be?

My heart was pounding from that psychological rush of adrenaline which only comes a few times in a man's life. I had to know. I had to phone the station. I had touched death and lived. Could it be possible the Preacher Man had come back from the dead?

My palms were sweating as I nervously dialed the radio station. My hands were shaking as the phone rang several times. "Come on, answer it," I muttered to myself. My mouth was like parched cardboard. Finally a man answered the phone in a calm voice. "WYGR, may I help you?" I didn't know what he was so calm about. He sounded like one of those generals we'd get on the line in the rear. All Hell was breaking loose, you were getting overrun, your life was flashing before your eyes, and they're talking to you in a businesslike voice as if it's just a routine call. I moistened my lips; "Is that Vietnam Veteran still there?" "Let me put you on hold," he said. "No, I believe they just left the broadcast booth. Let me see if I can catch him. He may not have left the station yet." Anxious seconds passed before a gravelly sounding voice said, "Can I help you?" My heart was pounding in my chest. I could barely speak from the surge of adrenaline. "Are you the Vietnam Vet they just interviewed?" "Yes, I am," he said. "Were you with the West Coast Navy SEAL Team in the Mekong Delta in 1969?" "Yes, I was," he responded with a detectable trace of excitement in his voice. "Were you the guy we used to call the Preacher Man?" There was dead silence on the other end of the phone. "Why, yes I am," he responded. My eyes were welling up with tears. My voice started to crack and stutter. With all the strength I could muster I said, "Ar . . . Are you . . . the guy who used to sleep underneath my bunk on the river barge on the Vam Co Tay and tell me about Jesus?'' His voice was no longer controlled, ''Is this Mickey Block? Man I thought you were dead.'' Half-laughing, half-crying he added, ''Pervert Number One, they told me you were dead!'' ''Yeah, that's what Buddy Mercer told me about you!'' He said, ''Wow, we sound like the Grateful Dead!''

For twenty minutes we laughed and cried. Finally Dave asked, ''Hey Mickey, I've got to know, did you ever ask Jesus Christ into your heart?'' Words cannot adequately express the exhilaration I felt when I told how I had almost committed suicide in my bedroom a year before and how I had surrendered my life to God after I had a vision. ''Thank God,'' Dave said. ''Man, I'd just love to see you and your wife.'' I said, ''Any place, any time, partner.'' ''Great,'' he said, ''how about tonight? I'm ministering at a church in town this evening around 7:00 P.M.'' I enthusiastically accepted, even though Shirley and I would have to cancel a dinner engagement. He gave me the address and said, ''I can't wait to see you.'' We said goodbye, and I chuckled to myself as I hung up the phone, ''I can't wait to see the Old Preacher Man either; besides, I've never seen a crispy critter evangelist before.''

When I arrived at the church, I couldn't believe my eyes. The service was sardine packed with an overflow crowd of over 2,000 of the most excited individuals I'd ever seen in a church. I think we found the last two available seats in the house at the very back. The congregation was raising their hands and singing exuberantly accompanied by a live orchestra.

I was carrying an envelope containing a snapshot from 'Nam and a .50 caliber slug that Buddy had found in our PBR after the firefight. I handed it to one of the ushers and asked if he would give it to Dave. When I handed it to the usher, he took one look at the envelope with the strange bulge in it and gave me a quizzical look like, ''What is this all about?'' He turned and trudged down the aisle and through an exitway toward the front of the auditorium.

I was already feeling a bit out of place in that building with 2,000 plus strangers raising their hands and singing like there's no tomorrow. But the usher's look made me even more uneasy. I was concerned about what he was thinking—some stranger handing him several ounces of full metal jacket and asking him to deliver it to the visiting evangelist. I had to admit that it was a highly unorthodox calling card. A sudden ripple of fear shot through me. Had he dumped the envelope into the nearest wastebasket? I remember lowering my head and asking God to have the usher deliver the envelope to Dave. A few minutes later the usher came out of a side door, mounted the platform where a number of men were seated, and handed the envelope to Dave. When Dave opened the envelope and the .50 caliber slug rolled into his palm, the men seated to either side of him did a noticeable double-take which you couldn't miss even from where I was seated. A large toothy grin flashed over Dave's face. He gave me a high sign as much to say, "Hey Mickey, man I know you're out there somewhere."

When Dave was introduced by the Pastor, the assembly gave him a rousing welcome. There was an uncanny electricity in the air. The whole atmosphere of the auditorium seemed supercharged with expectation, like everyone sensed something phenomenal was about to happen.

In that same raspy voice I had listened to over the phone, Dave began to explain how God is in control of our destinies and how he divinely orchestrates the circumstances and timing of our lives.

He related specific events in the Bible to show how God miraculously intervenes in individuals' lives at the right place and the right time. He spoke about Jesus coming on the stage of human history in the fullness of time and how God had timed the birth of John the Baptist to coincide with the birth, baptism, and declaration of the Savior of the world. He shared how, often, individuals called by God are only vaguely aware of God's overall design for their lives and only see in part what He is doing. He cited Philip in the Book of Acts as an example. Just when everything was flowing smoothly for Philip, God suddenly altered his plans. In blind obedience, he followed God's instructions to proceed to a dusty road in a barren stretch of desert. Philip had no idea that the Lord was detouring his life to a divine encounter with an Ethiopian eunuch who would receive salvation and become a strategic instrument in spreading the gospel to the African continent.

He then told the congregation how God had been directing specific events and behind the scene circumstances in his life toward a glorious conclusion which he had not understood until this very day. He shared that as he began to prepare for this crusade in Grand Rapids, God had awakened him several times in his hotel room with a spirit of travail, yet he had not been able to discern what was transpiring. He had sensed that something momentous was building, but he knew not what it was until now. "Let me ask you a question," Dave said. "How many times in the history of the world has the Lord directed individuals to a certain place and particular time in order to bring to pass His divine purposes?"

No one stirred. You could hear a pin drop when he told the congregation in no uncertain terms that it was God's perfect will that he was standing before them at that moment in time. He told them about an unscheduled talk show he had unexpectantly been invited to that morning with a local radio station. And he told of a phone call that caught him just before he left which catapulted him thirteen years back to the steaming jungles of 'Nam. Every eye in the auditorium was riveted on Dave. They seemed to hang expectantly upon every word he uttered. I was awestruck as we listened to Dave's reflections of a calloused, hollow-eyed River Rat he had bunked under thirteen years before on a river barge half a world away—a

211

hardened young man who had vehemently rejected his Christian testimony—a man who could blow away a Viet Cong and sit next to the corpse a minute later drinking a beer in complete indifference. He told the audience how the brutal realities of jungle warfare had twisted the lives of countless teenage soldiers and how the hostile young man above him had escaped to the refuge of immorality, alcohol, and bloodlust to ventilate his frustration.

Then, after untold attempts to reach out to that same young man, a hailstorm of armor-piercing bullets and grenades ripped the life out of that combat veteran he had so desperately tried to befriend. The Preacher Man's voice began to quiver as he told the congregation how he had broken down and wept when he heard of the attack and how critically that young man had been hit and how he had asked God to save the soul of that gravely wounded man before he slipped into eternity.

As Shirley and I listened, it seemed that all the loose ends of a lifetime were falling into place—all the fractured pieces of my past were coming together. It was all so awesome and mysterious. I felt as if we were in a strange detached state, like we were the only ones in that vast sea of people, like Dave was speaking only to us. Hot tears were coursing down our cheeks. We could no longer restrain our emotions. I buried my head in my hands as tears streamed down my face. I no longer cared who was looking. I could feel my wife sobbing and trembling under the waves of emotions that swept over us. People all around us were crying and wiping their eyes, not out of joy but sadness. It was as if they had all lost a son or brother to the darkness and were grieving the loss from the depth of their hearts.

Just then, Dave rocked the congregation with the announcement that the man whom he had given up for dead was worshipping with them that very night! The voice on the other end of the line that morning on the radio station was that man. By the grace of God he had miraculously survived the living hell of 'Nam. The news was like an atomic bomb. There was a moment of stunned silence, then the atmosphere of despair exploded into joyous triumph. The entire audience was praising God as they cried and laughed.

Dave said, "Mickey, won't you and your wife stand?" Shirley and I rose to our feet amid a chorus of tearful cheers. "Mickey, please come on down." I began to limp down the aisle. Everything was moving in slow motion. People were standing, applauding, and lifting their hands into the air. It was as though their gazes went past me and reached into some unseen dimension beyond mortal understanding. The sound of 2,000 Christians praising God reached a deafening crescendo which sounded as if the host of heaven was welcoming us home.

I was light-headed from the torrent of emotions. I felt so strangely weak, and yet at the same time a peace and contentment flooded my soul. Halfway down the aisle I put my hands up to my temples. I thought I would pass out. For a moment I felt my knees beginning to buckle, but hands seemed to reach from nowhere to steady me. What I was experiencing was beyond my control, but there was a compelling need to reach the front of the church.

Through watery eyes I could see the Old Preacher Man come off the platform and walk up the aisle to greet me. His face was viciously scarred, but I could see his eyes. They were tender eyes filled with compassion and unconditional love. We reached out to each other and embraced like long lost brothers.

We turned to face the teary-eyed audience with our arms around each other's shoulders. We were two former soldiers whose paths had miraculously crossed. We'd each taken a different fork in the road, but God had led each of us to the same glorious conclusion.

We stood alone, yet at the same time it seemed as though we were celebrating a homecoming with a family we had known all our lives. And there was a profound presence of someone much greater than us . . . someone more powerful than the minds of men could comprehend, standing with His hands upon our shoulders.

After a lifetime of darkness, I was standing in the light of a plan so clear, yet so sublime. I was part of something glorious which words could scarcely explain.

Epilogue

The Vietnam Memorial in Washington, D.C. implores a wounded nation to reflect. The haunting roll-call of names chiseled in the polished black panels bare silent testimony to one of the darkest periods in American history.

It is a traumatic page from our past which multitudes have yet to come to terms with.

It is easy to pan those somber panels and conclude that it was all a terrible mistake, and leave it at that. But the lesson doesn't end on that note. Even the darkest tragedy can foreshadow a glorious conclusion. There is more to Vietnam than painful memories and shattered lives.

My story is a testimony to that fact.

For over ten years, I met weekly with other Vietnam Veterans in V.A. therapy sessions trying to reconcile my past and present. Yet, those sessions reached no resolution. Beyond rehearsing the painful experiences of Vietnam, we encountered only deadends.

According to government statistics, at least 800,000 Vietnam Veterans are still suffering from some form of "delayed stress." They are our forgotten sons whose adolescence was raped in 'Nam. Their average age is 40 years.

Hundreds of thousands of Vietnam Veterans suffer from chronic flashbacks, nightmares, and substance abuse. Their suicide rate has climbed to over 100,000—nearly twice the number of combatants who died in Southeast Asia. To date, over 250,000 Vietnam Veterans are incarcerated or on parole. The divorce rate of combat veterans is approaching the 90 percentile range.

But beyond the 3.5 million men and women who served in Southeast Asia, over 40 million Americans have a direct personal link with a Vietnam-era Vet. Many of these "significant others" have shared the traumas and tragedies of Vietnam. They've seen their sons and brothers and husbands wounded and killed. Many have suffered the backlash of 'Nam in other ways. The rate of physical and emotional abuse of wives and children as a by-product of the stress has reached epidemic proportions.

The majority of Americans know little of the hellish realities of Vietnam. A whole generation of teenagers has grown up with Rambo and Chuck Norris versions of the war where only the bad guys die. Millions have watched the Hollywood portrayals of Vietnam in graphic detail only to leave the theater with a deeper sense of emptiness than when they entered.

For too long, our society has forgotten hundreds of thousands of wounded and the deaths of more than 58,000 men and women—5,510 tons of bone and tissue, 154,000 pounds of brain matter, 75,400 gallons of blood—cold statistics which overlook the human factor.

But there is a changing mood in our nation. Now, after quiet years of repression, we can at least talk about it openly. America is taking her tentative steps to recovery. She gropes and grapples in her struggle to find answers. The journey is searching and sometimes agonizing, but there is hope.

And yet, that hope is not in cosmetic healings. Neither

does it end with cathartic reflections or painful reminiscings. It goes beyond the political platitudes and tired mor-
alizing. It reaches into the heart and soul of us all.

The ultimate answer to the pain and grief lies not within
ourselves. It doesn't come from secular institutions or man-
made remedies.

It comes from He who holds the copyright on reconcil-
iation. The deliverance from guilt and rage and bitterness
comes freely through Jesus Christ. My story is a witness
to this reality. My body still bears the scars of child abuse
and war—but I also bear His healing in my heart and soul.
And I am not alone. Many across our nation have laid
hold of this hope. Marriages are being put back together,
memories healed, and men and women released from the
bondage of drugs and alcoholism. They are finding for-
giveness for the sins of yesterday, and learning how to
forgive the injustices of the past. Multitudes who had long
ago given up any hope of feeling can now love and live
again.

They have found this healing through Him who empa-
thizes with the wounded and betrayed and misunderstood.
He above all knows what it is to be mocked and spit upon
and betrayed by an ungrateful nation which He loved and
sacrificed Himself for. He suffered the same indignities.
Yet, His love triumphs over all.

If there is a fitting conclusion to this book, it is the fact
that God can redeem something glorious out of the suffering. If there is a fitting epilogue to this story, it is
the living proof that Jesus Christ is indeed "the Way, the
Truth, the Life."

Those that have dwelt in the darkness can embrace the
light, for it is Jesus who said, "I have come as a light into
the world, that whosoever believes in me may not remain
in darkness." (John 12:46)

Biography

Mickey Block is president of Saved to Serve, Inc., a non-profit outreach to hurting Veterans and their families. After being severely wounded a third time while serving with the U.S. Navy Special Forces in 1968 and 1969, he went on to earn a B.S. from Grand Valley State and a Master's Degree in Clinical Psychiatric Social Work from Western Michigan University. He has had the privilege of working for the Veterans Administration, a children's rehabilitation hospital and abused teen gang members in Arizona, as well as director of a drug and alcohol outreach program to veterans in the French Quarter of New Orleans. Mickey Block's wife Shirley, and their three children Jodi, Bryan and Rocky, currently reside with him in Ft. Worth, Texas.

Glossary of Military Terms

AK-47 —A Russian assault rifle.

A.R.V.N.—Abbreviation for Army of the Republic of Vietnam

A.W.O.L.—Absent Without Leave

B-40 Rocket—A communist anti-tank rocket

Betelnut—A nut widely chewed by the Vietnamese which stains the teeth and gums a pomegranate red

Body bags—Plastic zipper bags for corpses

Boot—Slang for a new recruit undergoing basic training

Bush—The outer field areas where infantry units operate

Bush hat—A floppy brimmed hat worn for shade

Captain's Mast—A disciplinary proceeding at which the commanding officer of a naval unit hears and disposes of cases against enlisted men

Caribou—A small two-engine propeller transport used to transport men and materials

Charlie—Slang for "the enemy"

Chi-Com—Abbreviation for "Chinese Communists"

Choppers—Helicopters

Claymores—Mines packed with plastique and rigged to spray hundreds of steel pellets

Cobras—Helicopter gunships heavily armed with rocket launchers and machine guns

Concertina wire—Barbed wire that is rolled out along the ground to hinder the progress of enemy troops

C-rats—C-rations or pre-packaged military meals eaten in the field

C-S—A caustic riot gas used in 'Nam

C-4—Plastique explosive

C-130—A cargo plane used to transport men and supplies

C-141 Starlifter—A large jet transport

DD-214—Service discharge papers

Debriding—A process of removing and cleaning away dead flesh from wounds

Deuce-and-a-half—A heavy transport truck used for carrying men and supplies

Dinks—Slang for an oriental person, especially in reference to the enemy

EM Club—Abbreviation for ''enlisted men's club''

E.R.—Abbreviation for ''emergency room''

Flak-jacket—A protective vest worn to protect the chest area from shrapnel or bullets

Frags—Slang for fragmentation grenades

"Freedom Bird"—Slang for the flight that took you home after your tour

Friendlies—Friendly Vietnamese

Garrote—A method of strangling someone with a wire

Gooks—Slang for an oriental person, especially in reference to the enemy

Grunt—Slang for any combat soldier fighting in 'Nam

Ho Chi Minh Trail—The main supply route running south from North Vietnam through Laos and Cambodia

Hooches—Slang for any form of a dwelling place

Hueys—Helicopters used extensively in Vietnam

Humping—Slang for marching with a heavy load through the bush

III Corp—The military region around Saigon

IV Corp—The southernmost military region incorporating the Mekong Delta

"Jody Calls"—Cadence calls and lyrics sung while men are marching or jogging in formation

K-Bar—A Marine Corp survival knife

K.I.A.—Killed in Action

Klick—One kilometer

L.A.W.—Light Anti-tank weapon

LZ—Landing zone

Glossary of Military Terms

M.A.C.V.—Abbreviation for "Military Assistance Command Vietnam"

Medevac—A term for medically evacuating the wounded by chopper or plane

M-14—An automatic weapon used in Vietnam by American ground forces

M-16—Standard automatic weapon used by American ground forces

M-60—A machine gun used by American units

M-79—A 40mm grenade launcher

Nouc-Mam—A strong smelling Vietnamese fish sauce

NVA—North Vietnamese Army

O.R.—Abbreviation for "operating room"

PBR—Abbreviation for "Patrol Boat River"

"Phoenix Program"—A highly successful program run under the auspices of the C.I.A. to eliminate enemy officers and communist cadre by assassination or kidnapping

Pogue—A derogatory term for rear area personnel

Punji sticks—Sharpened stakes used to impale men

"Rock and Roll"—Slang for fully automatic

R.P.G.—Abbreviation for "Rocket Propelled Grenade"

R&R—Abbreviation for "Rest and Relaxation"

"Salty Dogs"—A drink made of vodka and grapefruit juice with salt around the rim of the glass

Sappers—Viet Cong infiltrators whose job was to detonate explosive charges within our positions

Satchel Charges—Explosive packs carried by V.C. Sappers

S.D.S.—Abbreviation for "Students for a Democratic Society"

SEAL—An acronym for "Sea, Air and Land Special Forces"

Search and destroy—American ground sweeps to locate and destroy the enemy and his supplies

Short-timer—Someone whose tour in Vietnam is almost completed

Smoke grenade—A grenade that releases colored smoke used for signaling

S.O.G.—Abbreviation for "Special Operations Group"

Starlight Scope—A special scope used for night vision

GOSSARY OF MILITARY TERMS

Stars and Stripes—An inter-service military newspaper

Striker frame—A stainless steel frame used to immobilize patients

Syrette—A small collapsible tube fitted with a hypodermic needle for injecting a single dose of a medical agent

Tet—The Chinese New Year

Tiger Beer/33 Beer—Vietnamese beers

Tracer—A bullet with a phosphorous coating designed to burn and provide a visual indication of a bullet's trajectory

U.D.T.—An abbreviation for "Underwater Demolitions Training"

U.S.O.—An abbreviation for "United Servicemen's Organization"

V.C.—Viet Cong

Viet Cong—The local communist militias fighting in South Vietnam

Web-gear—Canvas suspenders and belt used to carry the infantryman's gear

W.I.A.—An abbreviation for "Wounded in Action"

Willie-Peter—White phosphorous round

XO—Executive Officer